$\mathscr{M}$ORE THAN PETTICOATS

REMARKABLE
TEXAS $\mathscr{W}$OMEN

MORE THAN PETTICOATS SERIES

MORE THAN PETTICOATS

—⊰●⊱—

REMARKABLE TEXAS WOMEN

Greta Anderson

TWODOT®

Guilford, Connecticut
An imprint of The Globe Pequot Press

A · T W O D O T ® · B O O K

Library of Congress Cataloging-in-Publication Data
Anderson, Greta.
    More than petticoats : remarkable Texas women / Greta Anderson.-- 1st ed.
      p. cm. -- (More than petticoats series)
    Includes bibliographical references and index.
    ISBN-13: 978-0-7627-1273-I
    ISBN 0-7627-1273-2
      I. Women--Texas--Biography. 2. Women--Texas--History. 3. Texas--biography. I.
    Title: Remarkable Texas women. II. Title. III. Series.
    CT3260 .A53 2002
    920.72'0764--dc2I
                                                                    2002070859

Manufactured in the United States of America
First Edition/Fourth Printing

CONTENTS

INTRODUCTION
ix

SARAH BOWMAN
The Great Western
1

MARTHA WHITE MCWHIRTER
Sanctified Feminist
9

CYNTHIA ANN PARKER
One Who Was Found
21

MARY ANN "MOLLY" DYER GOODNIGHT
Mother to the Buffalo
32

SOFIE HERZOG HUNTINGTON
Mother Lode of Stories
43

SARA ESTELA RAMIREZ
Beautiful with Qualities, Splendid with Virtues
53

IMA HOGG
Patroness of Texas
63

JESSIE DANIEL AMES
Antilynching Crusader
73

MARY LOUISE CECILIA "TEXAS" GUINAN
The Notorious Hostess
85

BESSIE COLEMAN
Flying for the Race
97

BIBLIOGRAPHY
108

INDEX
113

ABOUT THE AUTHOR
118

To my grandmother, Jerry Melton—
a native Texan and the best storyteller I know—
and to
the young women of Texas

INTRODUCTION

Texas is often portrayed as a man's world—a place where guns, cattle, and oil are king. This book should help to challenge that stereotype. The women of Texas's past could be every bit as direct, every bit as determined, every bit as adventurous as the mythical Texas men we know from movies and historical novels. The women I chose for this volume tend to be extroverts. They lived large, toting guns, fighting in revolutions, entertaining strangers; one even formed the first feminist commune. And they did many other "big" things: raised buffalo and roof beams, mingled with giant alligators, wrote revolutionary poetry, flew airplanes, and rode "astride."

But one part of the myth of Texas is true: The women did exert a "civilizing" influence upon the people of this place. Several women in this book fought against the destructive forces of racism. Sofie Herzog Huntington doctored the poor, no matter what their skin color; Molly Goodnight befriended the Plains Indians, and Cynthia Ann Parker joined their number after being captured and raised by them. Jessie Daniel Ames intervened at a crucial moment in Southern history, convincing tens of thousands of ex-suffragettes to shun the Ku Klux Klan and put a stop to lynching. And for civilizing influences, none matches Ima Hogg, who saw in Texas culture a rough jewel needing only the appropriate setting, which she sought to provide.

Writing this book has been a journey into the hearts, minds, and wills of heroic Texas women. It has also been a journey into history. One way of learning history is to read a scholarly textbook from cover to cover—a way I have never enjoyed. Before I began this project I had written several social studies workbooks, but I had never counted myself a history buff. That has changed. There is nothing like reading a biography to reveal the drama of the past and nothing like a series of women's biographies to weave a backdrop for history's drama, for women are inevitably caught up in life's material reality. Women's stories can transform even the most masculine parts of history. How much more interesting the Mexican War becomes when Sarah Bowman, "The Great Western," is cooking mess!

Here I would like to add a note of gratitude to those historians whose work made this book possible. I have strived to write good, true stories, not necessarily to uncover new facts. I cannot emphasize enough the quality of works such as Jacqueline Dowd Hall's *Revolt Against Chivalry*, Louise Berliner's *Texas Guinan*, Ines Hernandez-Avila's dissertation (soon to become a book) on Sara Estela Ramirez, Doris L. Rich's *Queen Bess*, Virginia Bernhard's *Ima Hogg*, and Brian Sandwich's biography of Sarah Bowman. Lighting my way in the early stages of the project were more comprehensive works, written by the very scholars who, in the 1980s, prompted the people of Texas to explore and celebrate their women's history. Open a volume by Ruthe Winegarten or Mary Beth Rogers, and you will discover a veritable pageant of Texas women. I recommend the works of all of these authors to readers.

There were many Texas women who have earned a place in history but who could not fit between the covers of this book— women who built bridges and fashioned empires, who oversaw circuses and cattle, who stood up to Texas Rangers and rising flood waters, who founded labor unions and kindergartens. I encourage readers who enjoy this book to seek out their stories, for preserving women's history is a job for us all.

SARAH BOWMAN
1813–1866

The Great Western

*I*t was early in the year 1846. Zachary Taylor and one-thousand men were on a march southward from Corpus Christi. They were headed to defend the southern border of the newly annexed state of Texas and had trudged for more than two weeks. As the troops prepared to file down a steep embankment, a commotion of bugle cries broke out on the other shore. From the cloud of dust, a warning was delivered, "Cross this stream and you'll be shot!" The column of Americans came to a halt.

Suddenly a 6-foot-tall woman with blazing red hair appeared at the head of the line. Sarah Boujette had proven herself a handy laundress and cook in the Corpus Christi camp. Her husband, being sick, had taken the water route with the other sick and wounded—and the military wives—to the supply base at Point Isabel. But not Sarah: She wanted a piece of the action. Before the trek she had purchased a wagon and mule team to carry the pots and pans and army rations from which she made a daily "mess," and she traveled overland with the troops.

Now she was face-to-face with Zachary Taylor, one of her personal heroes. If truth be told, she was more than face-to-face;

she had a solid 4-inch advantage over the stocky commander. She proclaimed loudly so that all could hear, "If the general would give me a strong pair of tongs, I'd wade that river and whip every scoundrel that dared show himself."

What did she mean by "a strong pair of tongs"? This blue-eyed colossus may have intended a couple of things. Metal tongs for grasping and serving food were certainly part of any mess cook's supply; one can imagine that a strong pair, properly wielded, could inflict some damage on the assailed. But there was more to it than that. Just a year before, a new style had become fashionable in men's work pants. These new pants were being called "tongs." Sarah was ready to show the soldiers how to fight like men.

Electrified by her example and the language that she used, the men charged down the arroyo and up the other side unscathed. The Mexicans scattered, their bluff called. And the woman who had rallied the men past this first hurdle was soon nicknamed "The Great Western" after the first steamship to cross the Atlantic, eight years before. That afternoon she stood in the stream to help some of the less able travelers across. Sarah was ironclad, in personality and physique. And like a ship, she was most definitely a "she."

The Great Western was born in the wilds of Missouri in 1813—or was it Tennessee in 1817? Sarah changed the details each time the census taker came around. Either way, she was raised on the border between civilization and wilderness and had no formal schooling. Her business agreements and census interviews are never signed with more than an X. With a married name of Boujette, it's possible that her first husband, like many other Frenchmen in the West at that time, was involved in the fur trade.

Sarah's career with the army got off to a modest start in 1840. She claimed that she and her husband first served under Zachary Taylor in the Seminole War in Florida, though there are no stories of a big, bold, red-haired woman in first-hand accounts from that war. According to her they were recruited from Missouri by a captain named George Lincoln, who also followed Taylor to Mexico. Although there is no historical proof, her fierce demonstrations of loyalty to both Lincoln and Taylor in the Mexican War suggest that she knew them previously. Joining the Florida battle in her twenties would certainly have been in character; Sarah would follow the army her whole life long.

Shortly after the encounter with the Mexicans at the arroyo, Sarah's wagon arrived along with the rest of the overland troops at their destination near the mouth of the Rio Grande. The Mexican army had gathered across the river, in the town of Matamoros. During a month of uneasy peace, Sarah did laundry and cooked, as did a handful of other military wives. Meanwhile, Taylor erected a fort, later to be named Fort Brown.

One of Sarah's most famous stands came in the skirmishes that followed. The majority of the men had been sent to defend the supply post at Point Isabel, 20 miles away. Only five-hundred remained at Fort Brown to face the five-thousand Mexicans on the other shore. At five o'clock on the morning of May 3, 1846, the Mexicans began shelling the American fort. Most of the women immediately retreated to the bomb shelters to sew sandbags, but not Sarah. At seven o'clock she served breakfast in the fort's courtyard, sidestepping lit cannonballs as she stoked the cook fires, stirred the kettles, and served up black coffee.

The shelling continued around the clock for seven days. During that time Sarah carried buckets of coffee to the artillerymen stationed along the fort's walls and offered regular meals at her table. In the thick of the siege, one bullet passed through her bonnet and another through her bread tray. A long scar on her cheek was attributed to a Mexican saber encountered at Matamoros. These close calls did not deter her from service. She carried the wounded to the bombproof shelters and tended to their needs. She even asked for a musket of her own and joined the fray. Finally, after one solid week, the fighting subsided. The American army had held its ground, with only two dead and seventeen wounded.

The Eastern press was eager to print this story of the opening skirmish in the controversial frontier war. The fort was named after the fallen major, Jacob Brown, and Sarah Boujette gained another subtitle, the "Heroine of Fort Brown." The first full account of her patriotic service appeared, appropriately, in the Fourth of July edition of a Philadelphia newspaper. A story in a New York City newspaper followed soon after. The Great Western was the toast of the army and became a bona fide national legend.

After Matamoros, Taylor crossed the Rio Grande into Mexico and during the hot summer months marched across the Northeast Mexico desert. Sarah followed in her mule-rigged wagon, providing mess for twelve young officers. In late September the Mexicans and Americans clashed in Monterrey, with heavy casualties on both sides, but eventually the Americans were left to occupy the city. Sarah moved into one of the buildings, hired some young Mexican girls, and established an all-purpose lounge, restaurant, and procurement agency she called "The American House."

The American House was short-lived in Monterrey, as Taylor's army was soon heading southwest for the town of Saltillo. This was a larger city, taken without struggle. In Saltillo Sarah reestablished The American House and did brisk business. She was known for fixing grub at any hour of the night if a soldier came in hungry. The American House was, according to one soldier, "the headquarters for everybody." It was also, of course, a first-class bordello.

Sarah saw action in the next major battle, which took place a short distance away from Saltillo, in Buena Vista. It was a two-day, drawn-out, tooth-and-nail skirmish, with the apparent advantage shifting from Taylor's forces to General Santa Ana's and back. Once again, Sarah stepped into the battle to nurse the wounded, dressing their wounds and even carrying them off the battlefield. Once again, she brought hot coffee to the troops and prepared food to sustain them.

At one point during this two-day siege, Sarah was back at her Saltillo restaurant when an underachieving Indiana private dashed in breathless with the news that Taylor was whipped, the army bust to pieces, and the Mexicans on the march. Sarah hauled off and decked him. Standing above the sprawled-out body, she delivered a few choice words and then declared, "There ain't Mexicans enough in Mexico to whip old Taylor. You just spread that rumor and I'll beat you to death."

A different piece of news Sarah received from behind the line inspired a wholly different response. She was told that Captain Lincoln had been shot and killed. Amid the smoke and din of battle, she searched for his body. Afterward, the matter of selling his gallant white horse arose. When someone bid $75 for it, Sarah counted that an indignity and bid $200, with the plan of returning the horse to Lincoln's family at the earliest opportunity. Sarah's code of honor was not for everyone, but it certainly had its rigorous moments.

After Taylor's victory in Buena Vista, the decisive battle in the northern Mexican campaign, Sarah returned to her business pursuits. Revelries at the unofficial headquarters must have gotten out of hand, because a new decree came down: "There shall not be a drop of liquor of any kind sold or kept at the establishment."

Mr. Boujette had faded from the picture by this time, but Sarah was evidently not fazed by this until the following year, when the Treaty of Guadalupe Hidalgo ended the war. The troops were headed on to points west to defend travelers seeking gold and profit in California from Mexicans and outlaws along the way. The leaders decided that women not married to military men could not travel with the company. As the troops assembled to depart, Sarah approached the commanding officer for permission to follow in the camp, and it was then that she learned of this regulation.

Without batting an eye she rode up to the line and addressed them thus: "Who wants a wife with $15,000 and the biggest leg in Mexico! Come, my beauties, don't all speak at once—who is the lucky man?"

One brave private came forward and said, "I have no objections to making you my wife, if there is a clergyman here who would tie the knot."

To which The Great Western replied, "Bring your blanket to my tent tonight and I will learn you to tie a knot that will satisfy you, I reckon!"

Thus, for two short months, she became Sarah Davis, a legitimate army laundress once again. Then, on a march north through Chihuahua, they came across a well-armed party from Santa Fe, their ultimate destination. On the banks of the river Yaqui, along which grew peach trees loaded with ripe, golden fruit, Sarah's eyes lit upon a man fully her equal in size. In the words of one observer, The Great Western "saw this Hercules while he was bathing and conceived a violent passion for his gigantic proportions. She sought an interview and with blushes 'told her love.' "

Then, when the demigod indicated his willingness, she "straightaway kicked Davis out of her affections and tent, and established her elephantine lover in full possession without further ceremony."

In the throes of passion, Sarah dropped out of history for eight months. She resurfaced in the hamlet of Franklin (the future El Paso), an important crossroads for travelers taking a southern route to California. She had resumed her original married name of Boujette, as well as her bordello business. This made her, according to one historian, the first Anglo property owner in the West Texas town. According to another she was its first "prostitute of record."

Sarah seemed to have an aura that protected her from the hazards of frontier life. Indians and outlaws alike were awed into a respectful distance by her epic proportions and sexuality, not to mention her apparent willingness to use the guns she carried. She made do with the erratic availability of provisions and consistently gave an impression of kindness to Anglo travelers who stayed with her. Even her customers commonly approached her in a "polite, if not humble, manner."

El Paso grew quickly, too quickly for Sarah's taste. She moved, this time away from the army, which had descended in great numbers and brought with it a wave of civilization. On she went, possibly by herself, possibly with a man named Juan Duran, to the town of Socorro in central New Mexico. By the 1850 census Sarah was living with Duran and five girls with the last name of Skinner—possibly orphans of the frontier, possibly employees. The youngest Skinner, Nancy, was listed as only two years old; she remained with Sarah as a cherished adoptive daughter.

Less than two years later, Sarah was on the move with another man, Albert Bowman, a soldier at least ten years younger than she, whom she soon married. Together they arrived at Yuma, Arizona. Like El Paso, Yuma was a southern gateway to California, situated where the Gila and Colorado Rivers meet. Sarah Bowman would spend nearly fifteen years associated with the fort at this crossroads.

At first Sarah worked as hospital matron and mess cook for army brass at the fort. The journal of a commanding officer, Major Samuel Peter Heintzelman, gives testimony to the forty-year-old woman's capacity to intrigue, arouse, and infuriate members of the opposite sex. After months of scribbling observations of Sarah in his journal, including the disparaging remarks of others about her mess, Heintzelman agreed to subscribe and tentatively found the meals satisfactory, especially when spiced with the woman's comments on his rivals. But when he tried to sell his stock animals to her, their friendship, as it was, fairly foundered. Evidently Sarah could drive a hard bargain.

Then she played upon this poor, bewildered man's affections. Telling the major that some strangers in San Diego were laying claim to her daughter Nancy, she enlisted his help in establishing a hotel across the river in Mexico, outside of U.S. jurisdiction, where Nancy might be seized. Evidently, Sarah was more interested in putting some distance between herself and her customers, for she immediately slacked off on the mess schedule. "The Western is making a convenience of us," the Major wrote. "She gives us what she pleases to eat and spends the whole day across the river." He got over it. He had little choice; hers was the only such service in town.

Sarah and Albert moved around Arizona a bit, from Tucson to Sonoita Creek, still on the military gravy train. In each new outpost she set up a hotel. Then gold was struck near Yuma, and the two returned to the fort. In 1864 Albert ran off with a much younger woman, leaving the legend to her admirers. By this time Sarah had adopted several Mexican and Indian children into her household. She spoke fluent Spanish with them, teaching them to cook and do laundry.

Sarah often said that there was just one thin sheet of sandpaper between Yuma and hell. She spoke either of local morality or the sandy ground she scratched to raise vegetable crops for the hotel. Legend has it that she died of a tarantula bite—a fitting image of the end of a rough frontier life. Everyone in Yuma turned out for the funeral. Memories of her bravery in battle were second only to professions of the kindness received at her hand. She was buried in Yuma. In 1980 her body was removed, along with the buried remains of soldiers, to be interred in the presidio in San Francisco.

MARTHA WHITE MCWHIRTER

1827–1904

Sanctified Feminist

$\mathcal{L}$ife weighed heavily on the heart and mind of Martha McWhirter as she walked home from a revival meeting on a hot August evening in 1866. Death seemed to be stalking her family, staking its claim in their new frame house. Two of her children had died that year; her brother had also passed away. She worried about the souls of those who remained. They seemed indifferent to God's salvation. She had endeavored to teach them in a proper Christian fashion, but they were restless at today's meeting. She wondered how faithful her own thoughts had been in the ungodly heat of the day.

While Martha was thus absorbed in self-reproach, she heard a voice that seemed to penetrate the cloud of her own thoughts. It raised the question of evil—in her life and at the church meeting. Was the meeting today conducted in the Spirit of God, or was it the work of the Devil? Had her beloved children died as a result of her own guilty associations?

When she reached her house, it seemed strange and foreign. The idea that she might be in league with the Devil had taken root in her mind like an aggressive weed. All through the night, Martha

Martha White McWhirter

prayed for assistance. She asked God for relief from her downward spiral of doubt; she asked Him to deliver her from evil.

Martha rose with the next morning's light to begin her chores. She had had very little rest, and beneath the nervous energy with which she set about her work, she was physically and spiritually exhausted. At least, she hoped, the work would occupy her mind with dutiful thoughts. Then, as she stood at the dishpan, she was moved by a sensation so strange and so profound that she believed it was the Holy Spirit baptizing her into a renewed spiritual life. It was enough to convince her that the voice she had heard the day before had indeed been that of God.

Such spiritual "conversions" were not uncommon in nineteenth-century America. Martha was raised in a period of great religious revival, known as the Second Great Awakening. During this period many churches were consumed by the desire for direct experience of God's will and God's grace. A person's conversion followed a series of definite steps. It began with a concern for one's soul, followed by an inquiry into actions that might be taken to ensure salvation. Anxiety about the prospect of eternal damnation followed, and the final step was accepting the conviction that one stood justly condemned. It was only then, when one felt absolutely powerless, that he or she could experience God's grace and surrender to God's will.

As a good Methodist, Martha had probably read the works of John Wesley, including his *Plain Account of Christian Perfection*. This work provided guidelines for how the converted should act afterward. Wesley urged Christians to "sanctify" themselves by striving to "have a heart so all-flaming . . . with the love of God as continually to offer up every thought, word, and work as a spiritual sacrifice, acceptable to God through Christ." This would be Martha's course; she was converted and declared herself "sanctified."

Although Martha's conversion experience was not out of the ordinary in nineteenth-century America, her response to it was. From her dishpan baptism Martha McWhirter drew her inspiration to become a radical feminist and thus commenced to outrage the well-bred people of Belton, Texas.

Martha White was born in 1827 in Jackson County, Tennessee. In 1845 she married George McWhirter and joined the Methodist Church. Over the next two decades of her life, she gave birth to twelve children, half of whom survived to adulthood. In 1855 the family moved from Tennessee to the fertile valley of central Texas. In the small settlement of Belton in Bell County, George McWhirter became a merchant and established a flour mill. The Civil War interrupted the family's march toward economic security; like many Texans, George left home to fight for the Confederates.

Martha was fortunate. Her husband returned safely from the war. A hardworking, reputable man, he had been promoted to the rank of major. Back in Belton he built the family a three-story limestone house and resumed his business pursuits. He was able to

THE UT INSTITUTE OF TEXAN CULTURES, NO. 79-101/DAYTON KELLEY COLLECTION

The Sanctificationists, circa 1895. Martha White McWhirter is third from the left in the front row.

support the family in modest comfort. George and Martha stood side by side teaching Sunday School at the local Union church.

Martha was past her prime childbearing years when her husband returned from the war. But she ran no risk of pregnancy following her fiery awakening over the dishes that fateful August day. As one who had been sanctified, Martha concluded that she was obligated, or perhaps entitled, to refuse the carnal advances of her unsanctified husband. Such a man—given to reading novels in his leisure time—might call himself a Christian, but he had not given himself wholly to God, as she had.

One can imagine the astonishment of George McWhirter when his wife moved into a bedroom down the hall. And this was only the beginning of her all-consuming mission. Martha began to call upon the good church ladies of Belton. It made no difference to her whether they were Methodists, Baptists, Presbyterians, or Disciples of Christ. She gave witness to her experience and urged them to pray for sanctification. It took several years to establish, but by 1875 she was leading a regular prayer meeting in her home and in the homes of other sanctified women.

The women had essentially created a new religion. They decided that things spiritual should be left spiritual, not mixed with the life of the body, as in Holy Communion. This rejection of Communion was heretical to many of their churches. Martha considered dreams to be the workings of the Holy Spirit. The women reviewed their dreams together, examining them for possible signs.

While there was this wholly mystical dimension to sanctification, the women's prayers were turned to emotional survival at the physical level. According to one member, "the central theme of their prayers was for patience to bear with their husbands whose niggardliness regarding household and pocket money kept women always beholden for every small necessity."

The prayer sessions thus served the function of support-group meetings for married women. In the context of Christian spirituality, these women were discovering the personal implications of their society's rules. If a woman was unhappy in her marriage, she was encouraged to acknowledge it openly and take action. In 1880 Martha explained,

> I have always advised wives to live with their husbands when they could, but there is no sense in a woman obeying a drunken husband. If a husband should go to a wife and ask her for his sake . . . to surrender her belief in sanctification as we teach it, I should say for her to do no such thing. For wouldn't that be giving up all our religion?

"Sanctification" became something Martha taught on an intellectual level, rather than an involuntary experience a person might undergo. It entailed a set of realizations about woman's place in the world and stood, in a way, for a woman's ultimate freedom. She called the women of her group the "Sanctified Sisters."

Attempting to squelch the movement, the husbands of Belton banned the meetings from their homes. The women adapted by meeting at the new Methodist Church. One day when the Sisters arrived at the church for their meeting, they found its doors locked against them. But Martha was not one to surrender so easily. She led the women through an open window to conduct their meeting. Thereafter, they convened at the smaller Union Church, adding to its superintendent's woes. The superintendent was none other than George McWhirter. His church had been in steady decline since Martha's awakening.

One of Martha's original complaints about George was that he refused her a partnership in his businesses. Martha's solution was to keep a few chickens and a few cows. The money she made from selling butter and eggs was hers to spend on household needs. Not all of the Sisters were permitted this freedom. Weekly discussions and earnest prayers about this dilemma evolved into a radical new theory: Married women, they concluded, deserved to be paid for the work they performed in the home.

It goes without saying that when the Sanctificationists of Belton approached their husbands with this demand, they were roundly turned down, if not ridiculed. Martha recognized the need for a more practical strategy.

In 1879 Martha decided to contribute her egg-and-butter money to a common fund, marking the beginning of the women's communal ventures. A generous schoolteacher who had joined the prayer group contributed her savings of $20. Soon other women were contributing egg-and-butter money if they had it. On the strength of this backing, one woman filed for divorce from her abusive husband and moved into the McWhirter house. History records George McWhirter's conditional agreement to this arrangement—Sister Pratt could earn her board by helping Martha around the house—but it is likely that he didn't really have much say in the matter.

As the fellowship grew in number beyond thirty women, the practical dimension of their enterprises expanded dramatically. With money from their common fund, the Sisters purchased a loom and produced and sold attractive rag rugs. They began selling cakes and preserves, or hired out as nurses, according to their talents, contributing everything they earned to the common fund. While thus engaged in the larger world of commerce, they drew attention to their spiritual commitment by wearing plain, dark dresses with white aprons.

Some of their tasks were unconventional. Two of the women, with the help of their sons, cut trees and carted firewood and cedar posts to town to sell. Another Sister's neighbor had mentioned that her laundress was doing an inadequate job. The problem was that there was no one else in the town to hire. Belton's middle class was ballooning, with no corresponding increase in the servant class. The town indeed was short of laundresses. In response the Sisters concluded that no task was too humble for them in their sanctified state, especially if it furthered their independence from their unsanctified husbands. So the Sisters began to work as laundresses and to hire out as cooks and servants.

Martha's theory was that their lives of physical toil might serve to accentuate their spiritual lives by contrast. Still, one fact could not be avoided: The Sisters were living on the economic edge. The comedown in status caused tears to be shed by some of the members. It took Martha McWhirter's staunch faith to maintain their morale intact.

The sight of white, middle-class women engaged in servants' work vexed their former friends and neighbors. One townswoman noted her anguish over her neighbors' firewood business. It was not easy to lose friends to Sanctification. It was harder to lose wives.

One afternoon in the summer of 1882, John C. Henry arrived home to find fifty-five-year-old Martha with his wife and two other women slaving over washboards and basins full of sudsy, hot water. Henry, most likely drunk, hurled sticks and stones and was reported to have yelled, "Shoo out of here, yar old hens! Now shoo out of here every one of you!" One of the stones gashed his wife's forehead. The four women struck back, and then returned in the evening to protest their treatment. The local authorities arrived and arrested Martha and the others. They were tried and found guilty of "occupying Mr. Henry's premises as a laundry to raise funds for the Lord," perhaps the only women ever charged with such an offense.

Another incident reveals the violence unleashed against "the

Sancties." In 1880 two Scottish immigrants, Matthew and David Dow, joined the society, attracted by its Wesleyan perfectionism. Martha McWhirter had no objections to men joining the fellowship, but she had opined that it was a rare man who could withstand the rigors of the calling. Shortly after they joined, the Dows were kidnapped and beaten by the men of Belton. The brothers ended up in the Austin insane asylum. Their attackers were quickly acquitted of any wrongdoing.

By that time—the early 1880s—Martha's group had nearly fifty members, the largest it would ever be. Woman after woman had deserted her husband or simply refused him sex and control over her. Woman after woman had been removed from local church rolls. Children were a particularly sore issue, as most women took their broods with them when they left their homes. These young ones were subject to kidnapping wars, as husbands and wives battled back and forth. At one point a posse of husbands approached the McWhirter residence and fired a bullet into the door. Martha and her Sisters faced these years with intense prayer, tight-knit community spirit, and a focused dedication to their work.

At first, women such as Mrs. Henry who needed to escape abusive husbands found places to stay at Martha's or another Sister's home. Finally, in the spring of 1883, the Sisters raised the money for materials to build a house of their own on McWhirter land. Again defying convention, the women and their sons supplied most of the labor. Having their own place enabled more of the Sisters to find refuge from their dysfunctional marriages.

Within two years' time the Sanctified Sisters had built three more houses, all on lots belonging to George McWhirter. The beleaguered husband objected, but that did not, or could not, stop his wife. Eventually he moved from his home to a second-floor apartment in downtown Belton—and there he expired, alone, in 1887.

Through all his years with Martha, George had been a model of patience and kindness. His actions made it plain that he still loved Martha. And Martha, in her turn, loved him. But it was one of her tenets that she did not "go calling" upon the unsanctified, though she might respond to a summons or act upon her dreams. Martha received neither a summons nor a spiritual sign after George left and did not go to see him. The circumstances of his death shook her faith in her convictions. Still, despite everything, his will testified to their deep, longstanding relationship; he gave Martha half of his estate and named her executor of the rest.

Another husband died—the violent-tempered John C. Henry. He also left his wife considerable property. After successive additions of rooms and outbuildings, the centrally located Henry house was converted into a hotel. Several of the Sisters who were working as chambermaids in the neighboring town's hotel brought their expertise back to Belton. Initially, the town's ill will deterred visitors from staying there. But business soon picked up. In 1886, the year the hotel opened, Belton was becoming a prosperous county seat, complete with a courthouse, a women's college, and an opera house. The hotel stood across the street from the livery stable and the railroad terminal. It boasted good food and impeccably clean linens. Outsiders praised its services, and soon the town's prejudice could not stop visitors from staying there.

In 1889 Martha McWhirter's personal wealth totaled almost $25,000 in land, buildings, and equipment. The following year she purchased land worth $5,000. Never one to hoard her possessions, some of these holdings and those of others were incorporated in 1891 as the Central Hotel Company, owned jointly by the Sisters. They built a three-story brick hotel on the lot adjacent to the original Henry property and thereafter used the Henry property for their own lodgings.

Collectively, the Sisters owned three farms outside of Belton. They rented two and used the third to raise whatever food they could not grow on the lot behind the hotel. In winter the farm was the site of their rug-weaving operations. They soon purchased a failing laundry for $5,000 and used it mostly to clean hotel linens.

With all their ventures the Sisters worked hard. Some of the chores associated with Sisterhood were fairly strenuous in nature. It was therefore decided that the women should rotate assignments, spending no more than two weeks at any post. None worked more than twenty-four hours a week.

The principles behind Martha McWhirter's expanding operations were not found in any political tract, textbook, or tome. They emerged from the group's constant prayers and practical needs—and as a practical matter from Martha's personal business acumen. A later writer characterized the keys to her success as "a shrewd insight into character, a quick grasp of conditions, honesty, and a firm belief in the value of cash transactions."

The 1890s saw a softening of Belton's view of the Sancties. Their prosperity was difficult to ignore. Martha McWhirter contributed $500 in cash to induce the railroad to extend a spur into Belton. She subsequently earned the distinction of being the first woman invited onto the Belton Board of Trade. As a major donor to the local opera house, her name was carved into its cornerstone.

The Sisters were tiring of life in the parochial town, however. The women had become more sophisticated, wearing slightly more fashionable clothing and subscribing to various "worldly" journals. They could now afford the luxury of travel and took group forays to Mexico City, Michigan, and New York, apparently in search of a new, more stimulating environment. In 1899 the thirty members, including two men and several boys, sold their collective property for $100,000 and moved their society to a suburb of Washington, D.C. The community of Belton heaved one last, sad, collective sigh.

Martha White McWhirter, aged seventy-two, made the move with them and lived five good years in Washington before her death. In many ways she had, as Wesley recommended, walked the walk of Christ through those many long years. She had emerged on the other side of great persecution; a passion and a certainty greater than herself were her practical guides. And what a strange certainty it had been!

Martha was unconcerned how the celibate society might perpetuate itself over time. When asked about the future, she simply replied that God would lead them, as He had always done.

In Washington the women enjoyed various cultural offerings and frequented the halls of Congress. They resumed their collective farming on land purchased in Maryland. This land was still being farmed by Sisters twelve years after Martha's death, though their numbers had dwindled significantly. There is no later record; it is assumed that the commune faded away due to slow attrition.

CYNTHIA ANN PARKER

1827–1864

One Who Was Found

It was a bright morning in May of 1836, less than one month after Texas had gained its independence from Mexico. A band of several hundred Caddos, Comanches, Kiowas, and other tribes rode into the clearing surrounding Fort Parker, a cluster of buildings on an area about the size of a modern football field, enclosed by a stockade fence. The fort was situated near the Navasota River, about 40 miles east of present-day Waco, but well beyond the western edge of settlement at that time. Home to several Parker families, the fort had been a scant year in existence. It was well-designed to guard against attack, but on that particular morning, many of the men were at work in a farm field 1 mile away.

When her mother, Lucy, heard of the Indians' approach, nine-year-old Cynthia Ann Parker was probably ordered to help round up her three younger siblings. Cynthia had been taught strict obedience, and she also had been taught to hate and fear Indians. Her father, Silas, was the leader of a regional unit of Texas Rangers, whose policy it was to attack any Indian encountered in the wilderness.

Cynthia Ann Parker with Prairie Flower

The Indians approaching Fort Parker carried a white flag. Cynthia's uncle Benjamin went out to parley with their leaders, whose requests were suspicious. They sought directions to a watering hole, yet their horses appeared wet. They also requested food, which Benjamin returned to the fort to gather. On his way back out, Benjamin failed to close the gate behind him. His relatives watched helplessly as he was surrounded, then brutally gored and scalped. The camp exploded into panic as the fort dwellers tried to flee through the storm of Indians charging the open gate.

Cynthia's father was speared and scalped inside the fort. Cynthia and her mother fled with the younger children into the woods outside, where they were confronted by men with tomahawks. Through the din it became clear that the braves wanted to take Cynthia and her six-year-old brother, John. Lucy Parker said her frantic good-byes as she lifted Cynthia onto a horse behind a Comanche warrior and then did the same with John. Three other hostages were taken that day: Cynthia's first cousin, Rachel Plummer; Rachel's infant son, James Pratt; and a distant cousin through marriage, Elizabeth Kellogg.

Cynthia Ann rode all day, clutching the Comanche brave in front of her. The rhythm of the galloping horse, combined with the day's trauma, must have induced a mental numbness in her. At the same time the sun's rays were sending darts of pain through her exposed skin. The hostages had been forced to remove all their clothing. The pace that first day was relentless, as the Indians traveled in small bands through prairies and woods, streams and rivers, putting distance between themselves and the site of the carnage.

Finally, around midnight, they stopped on the open prairie. Cynthia's hands and feet were bound with leather thongs, and she was shoved to the ground. There she and the others cowered as the Indians reenacted the raid with dancing and yelling and waving of scalps, while kicking their prisoners and beating them with their bows. The next morning the captives' hands and feet were released, and they rode north again. Again they witnessed the dancing at night. Day after day the sun blistered Cynthia's skin, while hunger and thirst gnawed at her insides. She must have realized that the tears welling in her eyes were useless. The Indians had no more food to eat, nor could they afford to take the time to hunt.

At the end of five days, they had crossed the Red River into the prairie of Oklahoma, out of the reach of the white enemy. Cynthia Ann watched as the Indians divided up the hostages. She herself was claimed by the Quohadi band of Comanches, who would head west from the Witchita Mountains to the High Plains, where the rest of their tribe would be migrating along the buffalo road.

Cynthia was joining the most nomadic of the Indian tribes. The little girl was no stranger to travel, as much of her recent life had been spent in a Conestoga wagon. Born in 1827 near the Wabash River in southeast Illinois, Cynthia was on the move by age six. Daniel Parker, her uncle, was the fiery leader of a dissenting Baptist sect who wanted to establish his Pilgrim Primitive Baptist Church in the "promised land" of Texas. In the summer of 1833, thirty-four members of the Parker clan headed downriver with ox-drawn wagons. The caravan crossed the Mississippi, the Red River, and the Sabine River, reaching East Texas during the first part of 1834. The next spring they continued southwest, crossing the Trinity River to the headwaters of the Navasota, where they finally settled, on the very fringe of the western frontier.

Well-accustomed to travel and discipline, Cynthia was also no stranger to adult responsibilities. The first year on the Navasota was spent hewing a fortress out of the forest and clearing the fields for planting. A nine-year-old girl could have been put to work in several ways, including child care and food collection and preparation. She would certainly have been attuned to the urgency of basic survival in the often unforgiving wilderness.

In these ways Cynthia's childhood prepared her well for life among the Comanches. By the end of the five days' journey, Cynthia was probably ready to submit herself completely to Indian authority, just as her captors were ready to treat her kindly. The Comanches favored prisoners of her sex and age and tended to treat them gently. They believed that white women were prolific childbearers and had found that girls Cynthia's age were more likely to convert to Indian ways. Thus, although Rachel Plummer and Elizabeth Kellog reported numerous incidents of sexual molestation, it is not likely that Cynthia was harmed in that way.

The ride westward to meet up with the other Quohadis was more leisurely than the escape north. At last the warriors took time to hunt and cook, to provide themselves and their famished captive with sustenance. If it was a buffalo they killed, they would have shown Cynthia how to use the buffalo grease to ease the pain of her sunburn. Perhaps it was around a campfire that they decided upon her Comanche name: *Naudah*, meaning "one who has been found."

One can imagine Cynthia's emotions when the band arrived at the main Comanche village several weeks later. To be at last in the company of women! Cynthia Ann, or Naudah, was assigned as a charge to one of them—perhaps to a grandmother who no longer had children to raise, perhaps to a woman unable to bear children. This mentor had much to show the young girl, and the capable Naudah soon became absorbed in her work and slowly began to forget her former way of life.

Tanning hides topped the list of Naudah's new duties. The Indians used the brains of the animals they tanned to effect chemical changes in the hide, but tanning remained a long, fatiguing process of scraping with a tool made from an elk's horn, sometimes equipped with a metal blade. The leather was then worked into everything from clothing and tepee covers to water carriers and braided strips, saddles, and moccasins. There were many uses for leather, and there would be no end for the women to the labor of leatherwork.

Naudah also learned how to cut buffalo meat into strips, which would dry into pemmican. The Comanche women went one step further, grinding the dried meat into powder, using a mortar and pestle. The size of the mortars, large depressions found in rocks uncovered near Comanche villages, suggests that the wooden pestles were probably 3 feet long. The women must have used them standing up. The ground pemmican would be cooked up into a paste for the tribe to eat during winter months.

Comanche women were in charge of taking down and setting up the tepees on the tribe's periodic moves from one place to another. They herded the horses in from the pasture and packed and unpacked their loads.

In fact, the Comanche women also had a special role with the horses. Herds of wild mustangs, or *mesteños*, descendants of horses that had escaped from early Spanish ranches, were prevalent in large numbers on the open range. The Comanche men, known far and wide for their horsemanship, captured these horses, but it was the women who "gentled" them, using only their hands and voices. Naudah took pride in this skill. Much later, when she had been returned to white society, speaking with a man who she believed would help her reunite with the tribe, she made the comment, "Horses! That is nothing. There are some first-rate horses and whenever I get my hand on their mane they are mine." It is the only boast documented in the otherwise dejected, post-Comanche period of her life.

As Naudah, Cynthia must have found something inside herself that both pleased her and was honored and respected by her new community. Only four years after her capture, the tribe was approached by a white trader who wished to ransom her and return her to her family. The tribe refused his offer; when he insisted upon speaking to Cynthia, she refused to say a word.

At thirteen Naudah would have been approaching a marriageable age, and she was certainly the prize among the Quohadi maidens. Several years later she became the first bride of Peta Nocona, already known for his feats of war against the white man. In the mid-1840s, she bore him a son named Quanah. She bore a second son, Pecos or Peenah, shortly thereafter.

She was with her two children the second time white men came upon her. The year was 1851, fifteen years after Cynthia's capture. Some white men hunting along the Canadian River saw her and offered to free her. She shook her head firmly, pointing to her children and the legacy they represented.

Texas joined the United States in 1845, and as the 1850s drew to a close, the ongoing conflict between Texans and Comanches intensified. While most of the Indian tribes had capitulated to life in the Indian Territory, only some of the Comanches had, and certainly not the proud Quohadi band. In 1858 Texas governor H. R. Runnels funded an expedition for frontier defense involving the volunteer militia known as the Texas Rangers. Led by John S. Ford, their mission was to destroy any "hostile or suspected hostile" Indians they found, including those found in Indian Territory. Peta Nocona's bold deeds in battle made him the trophy sought by every Ranger in the South.

Texas military leaders were now talking openly of "ridding" the state of Comanches. Numerous Plains Indian villages fell victim to their fire. Peta Nocona's nomadic band retaliated with bloody raids on frontier homes, leading Rangers on a hopscotch path of pursuit. In the fall of 1860, Sul Ross led a Texas Ranger company into North Texas. Peta Nocona and thirty-five warriors were off on a trading mission when the white avengers came upon the rest of the band encamped along the Pease River. Naudah was nursing her infant daughter, Topsannah, or "Prairie Flower."

The day was windy. The camp broke up amid swirling dust with the first shots fired by the Rangers. Ross and his aide, Lieutenant Kelliher, followed two Comanches fleeing on horseback, one of whom seemed to be the chief. Ross shot and killed the man they believed was Peta Nocona, while Kelliher pursued the other. The horse wheeled, and its rider held up a child. "Americano!" she cried. Kelliher saw that she was a woman and, approaching her, saw that her eyes were blue. She was taken back to the Rangers' headquarters at Camp Cooper.

At first Naudah refused to talk and claimed not to know her American name. Then Naudah questioned the Mexican interpreter about her two sons; she was assured that they had not been among those slain. At the same time the interpreter planted the idea that Peta Nocona had been killed by the Rangers, an error Cynthia accepted as true for the remainder of her life. Naudah withdrew. She was, in the words of one observer, "oblivious to every thing by which she was surrounded, ever and anon convulsed as it were by some powerful emotion which she struggled to suppress."

All present at Camp Cooper believed Naudah to be the missing Parker girl, and they summoned her uncle, Colonel Isaak Parker, from 100 miles away. Once the colonel had arrived, the interpreter drew from Cynthia her memories of a house surrounded by a large clearing, within a short distance of woods. Isaak Parker said, "If this is my niece, her name is Cynthia Ann." Naudah rose, pounded her breast, and said, "Me, Cynthia Ann."

Isaak Parker took Cynthia to his home in Birdville. A photograph taken in nearby Fort Worth remains a remarkable testament to her initial response to capture. In the photo Cynthia's hair is cropped short, a Comanche sign of mourning for the husband she believed to be dead. Her well-worn calico shirt is open and her breast fully exposed to the nursing Topsannah, whom she holds loosely in her strong, meaty hands. Her light-colored eyes burn through the paper and through the centuries, a declaration of self-knowledge and resistance.

Texas newspapers exploded with the story of the woman "rescued" from "heathens." Cynthia sullenly rebuffed her neighbors' assumptions that her redemption lay in Bible studies and in the quick adoption of American customs. They dressed her in American clothes and kept a close and curious eye on her. Still, she insisted on sleeping on the floor. Several times she was caught attempting to ride off on a Parker horse to find her Comanche family.

One day a relative witnessed her at a ritual prayer. She drew a circle and a cross in the dirt, then kindled a fire on the spot, added tobacco, and cut her breast to add her blood to the flames. Finally, she lit a pipe, blew smoke toward the sun, and meditated.

Sometimes her meditations brought tears. Her uncle, quite beside himself, told her that if she learned English, he would enable her to visit her Indian family—a promise he did not keep. Instead, he made arrangements for some women of Birdville to take Cynthia to the Secession Convention in Austin. After the bitter proceedings, the lawmakers remained to discuss further business and granted Cynthia a pension, as was common practice with war widows or victims of circumstance. The attention she received and the acrimonious tone of the secession debate caused her to mistake the purpose of the "council." She felt harshly judged and feared for her safety.

Shortly after this episode, Isaak Parker asked Cynthia's younger brother, Silas, to take her to his farm 75 miles east in Van Zandt County. Still, Cynthia showed no desire to join the white culture; the open frontier just west of Birdville repeatedly lured her to attempt escape. Eventually, the rural Van Zandt women came to respect her strength and her obvious appetite for work. Many of their husbands had joined the Confederate Army, leaving them to manage the farms. In addition to performing heavy labor, Cynthia willingly learned to spin and weave. Her skill in tanning leather was widely noted.

Still, her sister-in-law's contempt for "the little barbarian," Topsannah, depressed Cynthia. What was worse was when the women made the sprightly child their sideshow, calling her "Tecks Ann" and encouraging her to prattle in English when they took her to call on neighbors. When Topsannah caught pneumonia and died in December of 1863, Cynthia entered a state of mourning that ended only with her own death.

Cynthia's desperation to return to Comanche life during these years is illustrated by her reaction to a Confederate agent who shared a meal at the Parker table. Having been a Comanche captive himself, this agent addressed Cynthia using the few words of Comanche that he remembered. Her habitually grim demeanor immediately yielded to animated pleas. Could he take her to her people? She could get them some horses to ride. "My heart is crying all the time for my two sons," she cried. How crestfallen she must have been when he begged off, busy with the task of getting supplies from Mexico.

Although Cynthia's gravestone cites 1870 as the year of her death, other evidence suggests that she starved herself to death early in 1864, after Topsannah's death. According to Charles Goodnight, Peta Nocona also died in the mid-1860s. He had not been a victim of the Pease River massacre; his servant, Nocona's Joe, had been mistaken for him. Cynthia and Peta's second son, Peenah, fell victim to smallpox around the same time.

Quanah Parker, however, became a renowned Comanche leader. His chosen last name honored his mother, as did his warrior creed: Throughout the last of the battles over the Texas frontier, Quanah charged his Quohadi followers never to kill a white woman or child. He surrendered, by treaty, in 1876, moving his people from the Palo Duro Canyon to a reservation in Indian Territory. In 1910 he moved Cynthia's grave from East Texas to his adopted home near Cache, Oklahoma. He died one year later and was buried next to her.

MARY ANN "MOLLY" DYER GOODNIGHT

1839–1926

Mother to the Buffalo

$\mathcal{M}$olly Goodnight heard the boom of the rifles that meant buffalo hunters were on the Llano Estacado, the "staked plains" of the Texas panhandle. She was surprised there were still buffalo to be had. Several years earlier, Molly had seen the herds on her trip west to Colorado with her cattleman husband, Charles Goodnight. But she had also heard of sport hunters killing as many as one-thousand animals in a month. And she had smelled the rotting carcasses on the wind. Molly was one of the first women to settle in this region of the plains and was a rare female witness to the savage buffalo hunts that left thousands of carcasses rotting on the plains.

By 1878 fewer than one hundred of the giant beasts survived in Texas, and the hunt was essentially over. One day that same year, Molly Goodnight, from the "JA" home ranch in the Palo Duro Canyon, heard the plaintive cries of what she thought were wounded animals and set out with her gun to find them. Had they been badly injured, she would have to put them out of their pain. But the animals, two baby bison, were not wounded at all. Not far from them lay two skinned carcasses, black with flies. The calves bellowed; they had lost their mothers.

Mary Ann "Molly" Dyer Goodnight

Molly had never seen buffalo calves at such a close range because their mothers usually protected them so fiercely. Her long cotton skirts rustled the grasses as she approached the beasts. The calves were skittish—after all, they were wild—but Molly turned away with her mind made up. The carcasses would attract lions and bobcats, putting the calves in further danger. She rode out on the range to find her husband and asked him to rope the calves and bring them back to the home ranch.

At first Charles opposed her. The elimination of the buffalo was, in part, what had made his enormous cattle business possible. But Molly did not give up. Though she was never domineering, she often got her way. And she knew her husband well. There was nothing the two liked better to do than to ride out together in the canyon to observe the wildlife. Surely he could not be indifferent to the bison. "Think of it as an exciting experiment," she told him. Charles agreed.

In decades to come, the buffalo would become the signature of the Goodnight ranch. These orphaned calves were the beginning of the first domestic buffalo herd, an important first in wildlife conservation. Equally important, they played a part in preserving the culture of the Plains Indians.

Mary Ann "Molly" Dyer was born to a prominent Tennessee family in 1839. She was followed by five brothers. When she was fourteen, her parents moved the family to Fort Belknap in Parker County, Texas. Forty miles to the west was a temporary reservation the federal government had set up for the Indians, mostly Comanches, who were "suffering with extreme hunger bordering on starvation" from the degradation of their hunting grounds. In 1859 an ex-Indian-agent stirred up raids and racial hatred on both sides, which led to much fighting. One of Molly's brothers died in these battles.

When her parents died, Molly cared for her remaining brothers and eventually became a schoolteacher to provide for the youngest of them. On the way to a new post in Weatherford, Molly first met Charles. She was traveling with an entourage of soldiers, for it was 1864, and the possibility of a Comanche raid was real.

Suddenly, on horseback before her was Charles Goodnight, already well known as a hardworking cattleman and a fearless Indian fighter. In fact he had been with the group of Texas Rangers who had "rescued" Cynthia Ann Parker from Comanches four years before. Ironically, years later he would develop a friendship with Quanah, Cynthia's son, while on the Palo Duro ranch. After the day he and Molly met on the trail, Charles made a habit of visiting the Weatherford schoolteacher.

Charles Goodnight was not the only man attracted by Molly's grace, intelligence, and good cheer. He courted Molly for five years before he was in the position to make a marriage proposal that the sought-after Molly might accept. He lacked formal education, but he made up for it in drive and ability.

He had spent those years away from cattle-rich Texas, driving herds into New Mexico, Colorado, and Wyoming, where the animals were more valued. After their wedding in Kentucky among Dyer relatives, Molly joined him on his new ranch in Pueblo, Colorado. Molly's three youngest brothers, now grown into young men, were invited to come along to try out the ranching life.

As Molly and her modest entourage entered the town of Pueblo, the first thing they saw were the bodies of two outlaws dangling from a telegraph pole. A posse had caught and hanged them without trial. For Molly, whose father had been attorney general of Tennessee, vigilante "justice" was anathema. In Texas she had lived as an independent, single woman despite the threat of Indian raids. Living with outlaws and lynch mobs seemed worse. She asked to return to Texas immediately.

Her husband had to scramble to make their new home seem more civilized than it was. He introduced Molly to another woman in whom she found what she called "human qualities"—evidently more than could be said for some of the local men. As Charles Goodnight's business enterprises expanded into banking, real estate, and mining, Molly founded the town's first Southern Methodist Church so that Sunday mornings might be properly spent in the worship of God.

Hard times visited the West with the financial collapse of 1873, coming on top of an already difficult year of drought. Molly went to stay with relatives in California while Charles returned to Texas to plan his next move.

Charles visited Molly in 1876, full of plans. A Mexican guide had led him to a gorgeous natural region in the Texas Panhandle. He had immediately recognized the wide Palo Duro Canyon as an ideal place to run a cattle ranch. He staked his claim and found a partner in the Irish financier John George Adair. All this backer asked was that the ranch be named after him.

Charles and his men started the "JA Ranch" while Molly was still in California. She sent Charles a message, telling him if he didn't join her out in "civilization," she would come join him at the Palo Duro ranch. When he did not respond right away, Molly wrote again, "I will be in Denver a week after you get this letter. Meet me there." Ready or not, Charles had no choice.

A travel party made up of Molly, Charles, John Adair, his wife Cornelia, and four others headed out of Denver in 1877. Cornelia, a hardy horsewoman, rode a large white horse the whole way. Molly chose instead to drive a wagon. At one point she mistook a patch of beargrass for a band of Indians on the horizon. Obviously, Molly still harbored strong fears of her nomadic neighbors.

The canyon where they were headed was once a prime Comanche hunting ground. Besides hunting buffalo there, the

Comanches had used the canyon walls to contain a herd of mustangs. In 1874 federal troops had slaughtered the mustangs and defeated the Comanches, ending forever their dominance there. It is appropriate that Molly's rescue of the buffalo occurred in a place so sacred to the Indians.

The party arrived safely at Palo Duro, and the Adairs left after two weeks. Though they had made the ranch possible, they put a strain on Molly's natural hospitality. One day a cowboy sat down at the dinner table, as their cowboys always had in Colorado. John Adair complained that he and "Lady Adair" could not sit at the table with a servant. As the cowboy got up to leave, Molly fired back that anyone who was good enough to work on their ranch was good enough to sit at her table. The cowboy returned to his seat, and John Adair took Cornelia to another table.

Molly cheerfully made do while Charles and his men built a cabin and corrals. He had brought some 1,800 cattle to the canyon on his first trip. Several outpost men guarded the canyon's opening to ensure that the cattle did not leave and that the buffalo they had driven out did not reenter the canyon.

Molly wholly embraced her new home. Compared to the sparse vegetation of the surrounding plains, the canyon was thick with shrubs and wildflowers. It was named for the palo duro, or cedar tree, which, along with the chinaberry and cottonwood trees, provided blessed shade in the summertime. With her house backed up to a canyon wall, she was protected from the relentless winds that discouraged so many plainswomen. Of course, there were rattlesnakes and other creatures to fear. One morning, Molly was brushed aside by a small stampede of buffalo. But there were innumerable delights, as well: the sociable, if pesky, prairie dogs, the brilliant-red cardinal flower, fresh wild berries, the enormous blue sky overhead, and the sun, every morning, as it warmed the ruddy canyon walls.

Molly's early training caring for her brothers served her well on the ranch. Though she never had children, she was maternal by habit and at ease with the ranch hands. The cowboys loved her—she was smart, attractive, thoughtful, and she could cook! She often rode out to the men on the distant lines to deliver berry cobblers or cakes. When the men came to stay at the home camp, Molly repaired britches and darned socks as she listened to their complaints or soothed their aches with home remedies. The cowboys began to call her "Aunt Molly" to express their affection and gratitude for all her small acts of caring.

Molly's popularity earned her the title of "Mother of the Panhandle: Darling of the Plains." Her influence, as well as her husband's strict rules, made for a well-behaved crew, not disposed to drinking or cardplaying. She was never too busy to sit down with one of the boys for a lesson in reading and writing.

Two artifacts attest to the men's affection for her. The JA Ranch cowboys saved their money to present her with a silver tea service, symbolic both of the "civilization" she brought to Palo Duro and of her enduring hospitality. Another gift she received was a tall clock from her husband, inscribed in her honor with these words: "For many months in 1877–78, she saw few men and no women, her nearest neighbor being seventy-five miles distant, and the nearest settlement two hundred miles. She met isolation and hardships with a cheerful heart and danger with undaunted courage. With unfailing optimism, she took life's varied gifts and made her home a house of joy."

One day, a cowboy presented her with something just as thoughtful: a sack containing three live chickens. Assuming that the chickens were for eating, she made a reference to the next day's dinner. The cowboy quickly corrected her. The chickens were for her to keep as pets. She later described the odd satisfaction of their companionship, "No one can ever know what a pleasure those chickens were to me, and how much company they were. They would come when I called them and they would follow me wherever I went, and I could talk to them."

Molly is said to have been a first-rate natural historian, conversant with the wildlife native to the canyon. Her days of solitude were spent not only chatting with the highbred chickens at home, but also on the trails observing prairie chickens and curlews and taking mental note of the succession of plants and grasses. She studied plants used in teas, tonics, salves, and compresses, learning when they flowered and scattered their seed and which seeds would grow where, and why.

All this helped her survive the fearful loneliness she experienced. She once said, "If there had been no outside dangers, the loneliness would not have been so bad." She was referring mainly to the threat of Indian raids, which haunted her imagination in the early years. Nature supplied other dangers. Her attentiveness to her surroundings was a matter of survival as well as enrichment.

Charles shared Molly's love of the natural world, taking interest in everything from turtles to cactus and frost-resistant peaches. Riding together on the open range, they must have had quite a lot to talk about. For such long excursions the traditional sidesaddle proved uncomfortable, so Charles fashioned a sidesaddle with an extra horn on which Molly might brace her knee.

Within a year of the founding of JA Ranch, Quanah Parker and his band began to raid the Goodnight cattle herd. Molly was frantic to learn that Charles had gone out to speak with the leader. She barricaded the doors to her cabin with furniture. But both were reasonable men, not the kind of men who had incited so much hatred in the past. Charles had never hunted buffalo for sport; he had only driven them out of the canyon.

In a peace talk Charles confronted Quanah with genuine compassion as well as political savvy. He told him that the

Comanches' quarrel was with the state of Texas, not with him. No, he was from Colorado. It was a "little white lie," but it made peace possible. If Quanah's people could not find buffalo, they were welcome to Goodnight beef, as many as two a day, to satisfy their hunger.

Molly eventually got used to the idea of Indians near the canyon. It was hard for her not to think of them occasionally as she was feeding the buffalo calves in their pens. Years later, after the buffalo herd had grown to a considerable number and the Comanches had settled in Indian Territory, Charles Goodnight invited Quanah and friends to return to the canyon for an old-fashioned buffalo hunt. It was an opportunity that helped the Comanches preserve the knowledge of their traditions.

At its height of productivity in 1885, the main ranch in Palo Duro Canyon had nearly fifty houses, hundreds of miles of roads, twenty or thirty large water tanks, just as many corrals, and two-thousand bulls. It had its own farm for producing hay, a dairy, and a poultry house stocked with a variety of breeds, a tin house, and a blacksmith's shop. The main house was a two-story wooden structure, with water fed through iron pipes. The mess house was a "large and very substantial" structure where young men did the cooking.

Improved technology as much as anything had brought scores more farmers and ranchers to the region, and all the trade that followed. With the invention of barbed wire, would-be ranchers did not need to find a natural barrier, such as the canyon, to contain their herds. And water could be pumped from underground with windmills, enabling subsistence farmers as well as ranchers to settle in the Panhandle.

But the depression of the mid-1880s squeezed large and small alike, and it forced Molly and Charles to leave the canyon ranch to the Adairs and move to a smaller ranch near the town of

Goodnight on the prairie. Named after Charles, by now a famous rancher, the town had started as a station on the Fort Worth and Denver railroad line.

Now approaching her fiftieth birthday, Molly was ready to return to town. She threw herself into the life of Goodnight. Much to her husband's chagrin, her house was opened wide to people of all ages from beggars to celebrities, providing a center of cultural and social life. She initiated projects to encourage conservation of native plants and to educate Texans about the buffalo. As in Colorado, she built a church, but Charles never joined.

In 1898 Molly's dream of founding a college was realized. At Goodnight College, situated just over the hill from the Goodnights' new ranch, the region's youth came to take junior-college courses. They could pay for their tuition with beef or by working in the garden and dairy that provided the school's food. Mary Ann Dyer Goodnight became "Aunt Molly" to an entirely new group of young men and women, nurturing the students as she had the cowboys. In 1910, however, a larger normal college was opened several miles away, and Goodnight College enrollment quickly declined.

The reduction in their landholdings forced the Goodnights to cut back on cattle, but they always kept the buffalo, increasing the herd to 250 head. The Goodnight buffalo herd gained international attention when Charles began breeding "cattalo," a hardy cross between the plains and pasture animals.

By the end of the century, buffalo had become more valuable alive than dead; Goodnight buffaloes were sent to the New York Zoo, to Yellowstone National Park, and even to Europe. Buffalo hides, mounted heads, and meat became novelty items that only the wealthy could afford. Of course, the herd that Molly had started was also a major attraction for passersby and visitors to their large new home.

At the end of Molly's life, her house was a combined museum and bed-and-breakfast. Indian artifacts—found, given as gifts, or purchased on trips to reservations—were displayed side by side with the objects from the ranching heydays. She gave many tours herself, a fitting finale to an eventful life. She had witnessed and participated in much of the drama of early Texas history; it was written in her days and years and in her memory, and she was happy to share it with others. Molly Ann Dyer Goodnight died in 1926.

SOFIE HERZOG HUNTINGTON

1848–1925

Mother Lode of Stories

*T*he St. Louis, Brownsville, and Mexico Railroad began laying track in the Brazoria area in 1905, about ten years after Dr. Sofie Herzog had arrived there. Sofie soon was doctoring railroad workers. From remote stretches of country, perhaps some wild grove of oaks, sometimes late at night, word would come to her of a raging fever, a snakebite, or some physical injury.

Wearing her famous divided skirt that made the local ladies of Brazoria, Texas, fume, Sofie would grab her doctor bag and ride her horse through the mud, mire, and brambles to where her patient waited. Every visit increased the workers' trust in her abilities, and they would hail her arrival with renewed encouragement to the ailing patient.

"Dr. Sofie's here. She'll fix you up, alright."

And Sofie usually did. At fifty-five, with years of experience and the best medical training available, Sofie had a sharp mind, a sure hand, and a few special tricks of her own. She had been a mother to fourteen children and knew how to comfort a person in pain. And since she had moved to Texas, her daily life supplied her

Dr. Sofie Herzog Huntington

with any number of tales she could use to amuse the patient and the construction men who clustered about.

Sofie's work for the railroad was unofficial; she was simply the doctor they preferred. Then, in 1906, the railroad announced an opening for the position of chief surgeon for the entire line. Sofie had taken pride in treating the rail workers and applied for the job. This "Dr. Herzog" was highly recommended by the local company officials familiar with her work, and the company brass was swayed. Dr. Herzog won the post. Only then was it learned that the doctor was a lady.

Sofie must have read the letter that followed with a degree of amusement as well as anger. In so many words the company politely requested that she resign from her post.

Sofie fired back, "I'll keep this job so long as I give satisfaction. If I fail, then you can free me."

And so she remained, until her death, the chief surgeon of the St. Louis, Brownsville, and Mexico Railway Company. Summoned to different stops along the rail line, she would clap on a hat and hop on a boxcar, take a train engine, or even ride a handcar—a small platform car operated by a "gandy dancer" pumping a handle up and down. Sofie kept up her local practice and her mannish ways and, by the end of her life, had established a sort of truce with the ladies of Brazoria.

The doctor was not a Texan by birth. Sofia Dalia was born in 1848 in Vienna, Austria, the daughter of an internationally known surgeon. She probably grew up in a well-furnished home in which German was spoken and children were encouraged to learn. She was just fourteen or fifteen years old when she married Dr. August Herzog, probably one of her father's protégés.

The young wife began having children right away; eventually she had six sets of twins plus two more! Sofie's fourteen children probably taught her the habit of never taking any guff, yet she never seems to have lost her spirit of adventure. In the midst of bearing and raising children, Sofie was nurturing thoughts of another career. Modern medicine had often been the topic of discussion in her father's house; she knew enough to talk intelligently with her husband about his practice as well. At some point she began to take this unofficial training seriously, observing surgeons performing operations and learning everything medical science had discovered by the 1880s. In Vienna, then one of the medical centers of the world, Sofie received the best official medical training available to anyone at the time, man or woman.

Sofie's husband was himself a world-class surgeon, and in 1886 he received an offer to work at the United States Naval Hospital in New York City. Sofie and the youngest children arrived with him in this city that was young, dynamic, and rapidly expanding, far different from the imperial jewel of a city that Vienna was. But the thrill of this dynamic city must have worn thin when August Herzog became ill soon thereafter. He died within three years' time of their arrival. Sofie would have to provide for her children in this foreign country with its difficult tongue.

She immediately turned to the field she knew best. Though it was uncommon for women to become doctors, it was not unheard of in New York City, where Elizabeth Blackwell had founded a Women's College of Medicine thirty years earlier. Sofie already had the medical skills needed to build a solid reputation, and over the next few years, her practice expanded.

Around 1894 Elfriede Marie, the youngest of Sofie Herzog's children, told her mother that she planned to marry Randolph Prell, a native of Brazoria, Texas, south of Houston. Now in her mid-forties and with all her children raised, Sofie was free to go where she pleased. Imagining the adventures to be had in such a place, she decided to close her practice and follow her daughter to Texas.

Brazoria may have been a recently settled outpost on the frontier, but it had a history and wore that history with pride. Its denizens were descendants of Stephen Austin's famous "Four Hundred," who had arrived in the 1820s to form the first Anglo settlement in Texas. When the town ladies learned of Sofie's credentials as an Austrian surgeon's widow, they assumed the town stood to gain a dowager fully equal to their societal criteria.

The real Sofie Herzog proved a grave disappointment to them. From behind their palm-leaf fans, the ladies of Brazoria could see that she was in the prime of her life; worse yet, she wore her hair cut short, in pert little curls. They were no less appalled the first day the newcomer appeared in her divided skirt, designed by a local seamstress so that Sofie might ride out to her patients astride her horse, not sidesaddle, as was the feminine custom. Her ringlets topped with a mannish hat, Sofie was a smart-looking horsewoman—much too smart, thought the local ladies.

Sofie didn't seem to care what anybody thought. Brazoria was a romantic land of ancient oaks draped with streamers of Spanish moss. One could feel the lurking presence of wildlife: bobcats, bears, foxes, alligators, and snakes. The men on the streets wore guns and seemed familiar with their use. This was not Vienna or New York. This was Texas, and Sofie decided she would do what she pleased!

At first the doctor set up her practice in a room of her son-in-law's home. It was convenient, as Elfriede could help her with patients when needed. The arrangements soon broke down, however. Mr. Prell, Elfriede's husband, walked in on Sofie as she was rubbing an experimental ointment onto a smallpox sufferer. When learning of the patient's ailment, Prell demanded that he leave. Carriers of contagious diseases were not welcome in his home. The breakup was probably for the best. Dr. Sofie built her own combined office and living quarters in town.

Prell then made a point of worrying for his mother-in-law's safety. He offered her a gun to use to defend herself from intruders. Sofie refused the gun in every way she knew how. She finally convinced the Texan, with a sly touch of humor, that a woman with a gun was bound to shoot someone, and she did not want that on her conscience.

A few weeks later she had a story to tell to prove her point. When an unwelcome caller had refused to leave, she had needed no gun. She had simply seized an iron from the fireplace and waved it about. From then on Sofie declared the poker to be her weapon of choice.

Sofie had good cause for eschewing firearms. As a surgeon, she had to deal with the harm they did. This frontier town bore frequent witness to brawls, showdowns, and shoot-em-ups, not to mention acts of self-defense and vigilante justice. No matter how it happened, the wounded always staggered into Dr. Sofie's office for help.

The constant fusillade astounded the European doctor. She seems to have developed her own technique for extracting lead from flesh. Local legend says that she never probed a wound; rather, she noted the direction of the missile's entry and strung the patient in traction to allow gravity to dislodge it. Proud of her skill in this field, she began to collect the bullets she removed, saying that they were her good luck charms. After she had gathered a number of them, she took them to a jeweler to be made into a necklace. Each new slug she removed became a part of the chain. She wore it frequently and asked that it be buried with her.

Sofie collected many other things, as well. This was a land seething with mammals and exotic reptiles, and Sofie loved every one of them. She had every specimen she could obtain tanned, stretched, stuffed, or mounted for display in her office. In addition she had walking sticks from around the world and a trove of out-dated medical tools later donated to the University of Texas Medical School at John Sealy Hospital in Galveston.

Perhaps her most unusual collection was the shelf of jars containing still-born fetuses preserved in alcohol. One is said to have been a child born with two heads and three arms. Sofie said she kept them for scientific reasons, but one could imagine their presence might have disturbed some visitors to her office. When Sofie passed away and her granddaughter moved into the building, she took the jars off the shelf and buried the collection under a tree.

Dr. Sofie had a special relationship with some of the local young black men. Whenever they killed a snake, they would bring it to Sofie for a small reward. Sofie liked to string the snake on the side of the buggy house and skin it herself. When the skin was dried, she mounted it on a wide, red satin ribbon to hang in her office.

Once when she was busy skinning a rattler, her well-meaning son-in-law tried to intervene. The carcass still contained venom and Sofie might get poisoned, he said. Sofie, of course, laughed him off. In the days that followed, however, a puffy rash spread over her body and around her mouth. It took a trip to a specialist in Houston to convince her that she might think twice before messing with rattlesnakes, even dead rattlesnakes.

For a long time there was one type of reptile missing from her collection. Accordingly, Sofie hired a local African American to bring her an alligator from the swamp. The man appeared one afternoon dragging a 7-foot monster through her door. After taking time to give his feat due appreciation, Sofie returned her attention to her medical practice, stepping over the presumably dead gator several times as she bustled about the office.

Long after she had retired to the adjacent room for the evening, Sofie heard a resounding crash from the office. Holding her lamp overhead, she shoved open the door and gasped. In the dim, flickering light, she could see that the alligator in her office was quite alive.

Sofie now cringed to think how near she had been to its powerful jaws and enormous incisors. Grabbing the poker and shovel from her bedroom fireplace, she climbed atop her four-poster bed and stood there until dawn, watching the beast in stricken wonder through the open door of her office. It's not certain who finally killed it, but the alligator was stuffed, providing the good doctor numerous occasions to repeat her amusing story.

Alligators were then plentiful in the bayous of the South, and Sofie, like many other women, owned an alligator handbag. Hers differed from theirs, however. It was made from a very young alligator, with feet and claws intact.

Despite her skill at keeping the Brazoria matrons in a constant state of shock, Sofie also enjoyed the more conventional domestic pleasures of knitting and crochet work. In her spare moments between patients, she would grab her knitting from her workbasket to make scarves, shawls, and afghans for her growing brood of grandchildren. Three of those were her daughter Elfriede's children; others lived as far away as Mexico City and were known to her mostly through the mail. Her contemporaries said that she loved to talk about her grandchildren and followed their lives with "fervent joy."

Besides being a devoted grandmother and doctor, Sofie developed a third career. In 1907 she invested in some lots in town and quickly became a Brazoria real estate mogul. She attained such status as a businesswoman that an out-of-town land development company asked her to erect a hotel to accommodate the Northerners who came to the area to consider a land purchase. Sofie built "The Southern," a grand frame building across the street from her office.

Of course, nothing Sofie did was without incident, and the hotel was no exception. At the opening-day celebration, a wife of a former railroad employee confronted Sofie at gunpoint because she somehow believed her responsible for her husband's being fired. The gun's discharge sent the guests fleeing, but Sofie, unharmed, relished the scene. The bullet had whizzed over her head and buried itself in the wall behind her. That may have been one bullet the doctor did not dislodge.

Sofie had been raised a Catholic and was for a few years a devout member of the Brazoria parish. Then she determined that something must be done about the cemetery, which was overgrown with weeds. The priest was slow to admit that anything was wrong at all. The situation obviously began to distress her, and, having ordered some new fencing, one day she gathered some men to remove the old, rotting pickets surrounding each grave. The priest and some of his more loyal parishioners caught wind of her doings and showed up to demand a stop to the "desecration." Sofie, a great student of human nature, spared no words in stating her impressions of them.

Within a few months Sofie had joined the Episcopalian church to which her daughter's family belonged and had pledged to build and outfit a new church building for them. The church Sofie built was used until 1932, when a hurricane destroyed it.

Sofie was in her sixties when she became one of the first people in town to buy an automobile. Her friends mocked the idea of a woman her age riding about in such a newfangled contraption. But the horse and buggy had always been inconvenient, and after a few lessons from the salesman, Sofie began to make her rounds in a Ford runabout, tooting her horn in greeting at those she met. Little had changed from the days when she had ridden her horse down the road in her scandalous divided skirt.

It was about that time in her life that this independent woman found a man with whom to spend the rest of her life. Evidently some of the old-timers had grown to appreciate her ways, for the seventy-year-old bridegroom, Colonel Marion Huntington, was a descendant of the Austin Four Hundred. Little record of their relationship exists. The fact that Sofie deeded much of her real estate to her daughter two years before the wedding might indicate the courtship was a long one, for under the law as it then existed, all of Sofie's property would have belonged to her husband after the marriage.

Though marriage might have restricted her legal rights, it did nothing to diminish Sofie's spirit. On her marriage certificate she crossed out "Miss" and "Mrs." and scribbled in "Dr." Her husband did not interfere with her practice; she simply became "Dr. Sofie Herzog Huntington" to her patients. Sofie moved to her husband's plantation 7 miles out of town and drove her car into town every day. She remained active until her death in 1925.

Despite all of her wild eccentricities, Sofie was a professional woman in a man's world. She attended medical conventions and often spoke at them. She also defied the racial prejudice of the time, delivering the babies of black women who lived along the Brazos River. Dr. Sofie would have been remarkable without her curiosities. It is a boon that her life and doings gave rise to such a mother lode of stories, which have been circulated and revived several times in all of the local papers. She is still a celebrity in Brazoria, where a small museum has been dedicated to a display of her fascinating artifacts.

SARA ESTELA RAMIREZ

1881–1910

Beautiful with Qualities, Splendid with Virtues

*T*he "muse of Texas mourned" at the death of twenty-nine-year-old Sara Estela Ramirez. Such was the claim of one of her obituaries. Sara was "a profound thinker and forceful writer," "the first of the woman poets of the region"; she "knew how to make known the beautiful sentiments that she harbored in her noble and generous heart."

Of the four surviving eulogies of Sara Estela Ramirez, none is more eloquent than that of her friend and colleague Jovita Idar, a writer whose father owned *La Crónica,* an alternative newspaper for the Spanish-speaking community in Laredo. Jovita was still a girl when the newspaper first began publishing Sara's poems, so full of beautiful ideals, painful truths, and passionate expressions of sisterhood. By the time of her death ten years later, Sara Estela—a teacher of great intelligence, a first-class poet, and an outspoken friend of Mexico's revolutionary movement—had become an important model for Jovita, a teacher, writer, and revolutionary herself. Here is what Jovita wrote on her death:

Sara Estela has not died. The memory of her exemplary life will endure always latent in those of us who came to know her elevated and noble character and [who came] to perceive something of the luminous reflection of her cultivated intelligence and her tender heart.

Upon losing her, materially, we have lost not the friend, but the sister and the mentor, since her sweet and persuasive voice never was heard in vain conversations, but rather it was always quick to impart to us from the abundance of the vast knowledge that she possessed. . . .

I also lament her separation because united by the most intimate ties of affection, always firm and lasting, her name was the synonym of true and intimate friendship, and of what is most loving and selfless in the human spirit.

Let us not cry for her; her sweet name and the memory of her life will remain among us, as an example of the most elevated feelings, of her immaculate patriotism, and unwavering love and sympathy for all of us who cultivated her friendship. . . .

Who was this melodious songbird, this immaculate patriot and altruist? Besides the eulogies most of what we know of Sara comes from what has survived of her writings: twenty or so poems, a speech, and several letters, all in Spanish. There are no photographs, no physical descriptions. She never married or had children. Yet her poems paint a vivid portrait of a unique and profound individual.

Sara Estela Ramirez was born in 1881 in Villa de Progreso, a small town on the Salado River in Coahuila, Mexico. When she was still very young, her mother died, leaving her and her younger sister, María, in the care of their father. Sara remained very close to these two her whole life, soon adopting her mother's caretaking roles. She received her primary education in Monterrey, and then her teacher's training, with high praise, from the Ateneo Fuentes in Saltillo. During these years a passion for learning must have been kindled in Sara, who received acclaim from Clemente Idar, Jovita's father, as well as from Jovita for her possession of "vast knowledge."

When she was about sixteen, Sara moved to Laredo, Texas, with her sister María. This South Texas border town had been growing rapidly, both in population and sophistication. The newly constructed railroad linked centers of business in Texas and Mexico, making Laredo a crossroads of the new capitalist economy. Railroads and mines were the major industries in the region; recently, their workers had organized themselves into labor unions. Newspapers like *La Crónica* played an important role in the heightened political consciousness of the Mexican working class and other Mexicans in the region.

Sara became a Spanish teacher at the Semanario in Laredo. This secondary school, established for Texans of Mexican background, may have been a project of the Idars and their partners. Her students there were girls, primarily from comfortable, middle-class backgrounds. Sara was known as a gifted and self-sacrificing teacher, who "distributed prodigiously the light of her intelligence, fertilizing thousands of young minds." Lines from a prose poem about one particularly impoverished student attest to Sara's intense emotional involvement in her work: "More than one time I accompanied María to her house. Such humility, such poverty, better said, such misery!" Yet Sara's concern for this underprivileged girl was not a form of pity or piety, but of true empathy. In the sadness of the student, who had lost her father, Sara saw an image of her own "blacknesses," as she called them, and she felt connected to the girl: "Her being an orphan and my being an orphan made us sisters, her misery was also mine, her sorrow my sorrow."

In the poem the innocent love of this schoolgirl saves Sara from the "hammer" of obsessive, self-destructive thoughts. Walking along briskly, the poem's speaker has forgotten herself, forgotten María beside her, and accidentally hits her with her swinging hand. María does not complain, but kisses the hand tenderly. "The darkness of that day had a ray of light: I came back to myself, I thought of her with infinite tenderness, with unspeakable love; and upon smiling at her, I blessed the heaven that gives us the kiss of an angel for the dark hours of life."

Soon after *La Crónica* began publishing Sara's poems, the editors of *La Regeneración*, the newspaper that served the resistance movement in Mexico, praised her writing and offered her a complimentary subscription. The newspaper spoke out forcefully against the hierarchy of the Catholic Church and against Porfirio Diaz, who had been dictator of Mexico since 1876. In May of 1901 Sara wrote the first of what would be a series of letters to Ricardo Flores Magón, leader of the resistance movement, thanking him for the subscription and extolling "the bold civic valor that characterize[d]" the newspaper. Too many people, she complained, allow their fears of reprisal to silence the criticisms they feel so keenly. She vowed to begin her own liberal journal, called *La Corregidora*, dedicating to the cause "the little energies of her life."

The name of Sara's journal is very significant. *La Corregidora* translates as "The Magistrate's Wife" and refers to a heroine of the Mexican War for Independence of 1810. Doña Josefa Ortíz de Dominguez was a Creole, of mixed Spanish and native blood, famous for using her unofficial power to assist revolutionaries. As a woman, Sara occupied an unofficial but important role in the new movement. In that first letter to Magón, she argued that in Laredo "the woman is the most mobile and most powerful lever" for social change. It was true—in many cases, women doing party work could escape the ever-increasing harassment that high-profile males received from the Mexican military. Safely outside of Mexican jurisdiction, Sara and other women linked resistors in Mexico with those who found refuge in exile in Texas. This women's auxiliary called itself *Regeneración y Concordia,* "Renewal and Harmony."

Besides the end of dictatorship, the opposition focused on the conditions of peasants and the working-class poor. New agriculture policies had entitled outsiders to dispossess the peasant farmers, or *campesinos,* of their lands. Conditions were no better in the cities, where workers received subsistence wages in coupons redeemable only at company stores. Porfirio Diaz used military force to quell outbreaks of rebellion. In the meantime he consorted with the conservative leadership of the Mexican Catholic Church and with ideologues whose views reinforced the status quo. One such pet philosopher was Andres Molina Enriquez, who used quasi-scientific reasoning to "prove" the biological inferiority of women. Opposing viewpoints were routinely repressed through arrest and harassment.

It's not surprising that schoolteachers were among those most affected by the "Porfiriato," as this period was called; during Diaz's rule their real wages declined to the level of a household servant's pay. With their abilities, women like Sara became spokeswomen and organizers for the nascent revolution. But because she was a poet, Sara took on a unique role as a kind of spiritual guide. Though removed from the action because she lived in Texas, she experienced deeply the hopes and setbacks of the group and expressed the experience in beautiful, ennobling language.

Within two years of the first letter, Sara and Magón had become close friends. Their correspondence blossomed in 1903, Magón's last year in Mexico. In one letter Sara hears of discord among what she calls "the pleiade of heroic patriots." She asks Magón for details, adding, "Until you inform me of all that, I only beg my brother that we unite once again, leaving the past behind and putting aside our childishness. We are all subject to error; no one is perfect."

The troubles did not go away, especially as the Diaz government kept up its harassment tactics. In her December 1903 letter to Magón, Sara wrote,

My beloved brother:

If I tell you that my days are black and continue to be black, I will tire you, although my blacknesses have become, as Juanita says, proverbial. . . .

My black hours increase . . . with the sad situation we are all in. I think about my dear imprisoned, ill sisters, and my heart hurts not to be able to help them. I think about you and the other young associates who have recently been given their freedom and my soul hurts to see the struggle they sustain against such fatal circumstances that surround us.

Two months later Magón and others came to Sara in Laredo when they were forced to flee Mexico, their press confiscated and their very lives in danger. Their arrival aroused in her dreams of "beautiful projects for the future." But within a short time, she became "disillusioned with everything, absolutely everything." What happened is not clear, but one month later, she had moved to San Antonio, the new publishing headquarters of *La Regeneración*. With her there was Camilo Arriaga, a well-off movement backer who opposed some of Magón's more radical anarchist beliefs. Meanwhile, Magón was in St. Louis with the group that would found the Mexican Liberal Party in 1906. The *Magónistas*, as they were called, helped significantly to prepare the way for the Revolution of 1911.

From San Antonio Sara wrote to Magón of her disappointments, concluding her letter, "I will try for my part to keep my heart immaculate to practice good and to love always very much, perhaps more than now, the people, the little people as you call them, and be sure, my dear brother, that I will struggle for them, always for them." There is no evidence that she ever broke this vow.

The need for unity in political resistance was the message of Sara's one surviving speech. In this speech to the Society of Workers in April of 1909, she defined the most winning characteristic of the workers' movement as *mutualismo.* "Mutualism," she said, "needs hearts that say: I am for you, as I want you to be for me, mutualism has need of us workers, the humble, the small gladiators of the idea, it needs for us to salvage from our egotisms something immense, something divine, that can make us a society, that can make us nobly human." Sara never gave up the hope that people could become better than they were, and she shared that hope with her audience: "And with your example may you show societies how to love each other . . . and to unite so that they may be strong."

Unity and love, or *mutualismo,* was one of Sara's major themes, but the idea of overcoming great emotional obstacles occupies an even larger place in her writings. Her poems suggest that Sara fought a lifelong battle with despair. The source of these "blacknesses" can only be guessed, but the poems and letters hint at several causes. From her letters it is clear that her family and particularly her father, Jesus María, opposed her involvement in the opposition movement. Estrangement from her family must have caused her great grief. In addition, Sara faced death daily. She writes of how her infant nephew died of dengue fever, a tropical disease carried by mosquitoes. When she was twenty she had apologized for her "little energies"; a contemporary describes her as having suffered "a slow sickness that took her to her grave."

Finally, her poems chronicle an unrequited love of the most intense form, such as the following passage from "Ambition":

I would like to know if you have dreamt
As I have dreamt
I would like to know if in me you have found
What in your love I have found;
I would like to be everything you have loved,
Everything you have dreamed I want to be,
Just as you are everything I love,
Everything I have dreamed of . . .

The love was apparently not mutual. The fruitlessness of her dreams is given form in "Blank Page," a poem that tells of how the speaker's album of past loves contains one blank page:

None to my eyes
Is so sweet and so sad as this one.
And do you know why? Yes, you know.
You understand sublime loves!
That page was for you or for no one;
You did not write? . . . Let no one touch it.

During her twenties Sara devoted her energies to various overlapping organizations and publications of the resistance movement. She organized for the Mexican Liberal Party, participated in *Club Redención,* an anticlerical group, and remained a close colleague of the women who founded *Regeneración y Concordia.* She gave up her newspaper, *La Corregidora,* in 1903, but she contributed poems to alternative newspapers such as *El Demócrata Fronterizo* and *La Crónica.* It is significant that these papers included space for poetry; it suggests the movement's optimism, creativity, and inclusiveness. In 1910 Sara founded her own literary journal, *Aurora*, extravagantly heralded by her friends at *La Crónica*. A reviewer wrote that just as the dawn awakes the natural world, so *Aurora* awoke the intellectual world "with its magic wand of beautiful and select literature, . . . dispersing brilliant light on the foreheads of its readers."

The reviewer goes on to describe the author and editor as "struggling always against adversity." Sara's poem "The Struggle for Good" reflects this reality:

> The intense night of human passions inundates with its shadows the harsh and difficult path.
>
> And there go the travelers, poor blind ones! Falling and getting up . . . now desperate, now patient, now ambivalent, now serene and full of valor and confidence, searching always for the farthest goal!
>
> They know that a fall does not extinguish faith, but rather sets fire to experience, and experience is the light that illuminates the tenebrous night of human passions.

"Black Diamonds," a poem to a young "sister" named Yuly, expands this light-and-dark metaphor for the sacred aspect to suffering. From the "somber concaves" of despair, the author and her friend hear of "del bien," or of "the good." While pleasure, love, illusion, and hope all seem to be "prohibited," no one can deny "that the darknesses of our souls like diamonds give out light. . . ."

Such poems, as personal as they were, spoke to Sara's contemporaries. The struggle for light is a metaphor for the formation of a revolutionary movement to overthrow an oppressive regime. Certainly her poetry resonated just as strongly with the Mexican Americans of Texas, whose spirits were daily diminished by the messages of the dominant culture. But her poems transcend their immediate context. Anyone who has experienced feelings of true friendship, ideal love, and the struggle against darkness can find solace and inspiration in her words.

Sara's most spectacular poem is titled "Surge" in Spanish. It is addressed to woman, "a la mujer": "Rise up! Rise up to life, to activity, to the beauty of truly living; but rise up radiant and powerful, beautiful with qualities, splendid with virtues, strong with energies."

She goes on to urge women to reject the roles of "goddess" or "queen" on a throne, for "Gods live what their followers want" and rulers are dethroned.

> . . . woman always lives and this is the secret of her happiness, to live.
>
> Only action is life; to feel that one lives is the most beautiful sensation.
>
> Rise up, then, to the beauties of life; but rise up so, beautiful with qualities, splendid with virtues, strong with energies.

This paean to life was the last poem Sara wrote that we know of. She died in 1910, at the age of twenty-nine. But she already had risen up, beautiful with qualities, in the minds of her contemporaries, influencing an entire generation of women through her writings. It is tragic that only some of her body of writing remains to testify to her brief life and noble contribution. She truly was a remarkable woman.

IMA HOGG

1882–1975

Patroness of Texas

*J*anuary 10, 1901, was a momentous day in Texas history. From a lone derrick on a hill surrounded by rice fields outside Beaumont, mud began to spew, knocking a pipe loose and causing drilling to cease. For a while the well was quiet. As workers began scraping the muck off the derrick floor, they were showered by a roaring explosion of mud, followed by a giant rush of gas, then the highest plume of black oil the world had ever seen. The gusher at Spindletop confirmed every Texan's hunch and hope that there was "black gold" underground for the taking.

Former Texas governor James Stephen Hogg was among the first to join the gold rush, purchasing mineral rights to fifteen acres of adjacent ground, which he easily leased out to prospectors. Within a year he had joined others to form the Texas Company, soon known as Texaco. But the Hogg family had not yet joined the ranks of the extraordinarily rich. Boom times actually kept prices depressed with an oversupply of oil. Meanwhile, Mr. Hogg waited for riggers to drill on the family estate in nearby West Columbia. It was not until 1919, long after Hogg's death, that those fields were tapped and found to be rich with oil.

Ima Hogg, circa 1910

By this time another Hogg was in charge, daughter Ima. There exists a wonderful photograph of James Hogg's only daughter late in her life, supervising the restoration of a historic barn at Round Top, the site of an old stagecoach inn between Austin and Houston. She seems nonplussed by the country mud and construction materials strewn about her on the ground; her expression is focused in a critical assessment of the work in progress. With an iron will and a sense of humor, Ima Hogg labored to transform Texas mud into some semblance of culture. She spent her life and her considerable Texas wealth to bequeath this legacy to the citizens of her state.

Ima had to struggle out of a muddy slough of her own to emerge whole from her childhood. In 1882, when she was born and christened, James Stephen Hogg was a stump politician in a rural district. It was a time when the common man was ascendant in politics. James Hogg was, amusingly enough, a very large man, and he used his last name to appeal to his audience's earthy sense of humor. On his trips across Texas during his 1892 gubernatorial campaign, ten-year-old Ima was his mascot, sometimes joined by a friend. With a roar of laughter from the crowd, Hogg would introduce his "two daughters, Ima and Ura." Ura was fictional, but the legend lives on.

"Ima," however, was a reality, and a difficult one to ignore. When questioned, the senior Hogg explained that he chose the name from a Civil War poem penned by his brother and hadn't realized the consequences to his daughter until it was too late. Ima never shrank from her name; when introducing herself, she simply paused, ever so slightly, between the first name and the last. Nor did she ever abandon her father. After his death Ima vigorously disputed the unfavorable caricatures of him drawn by certain journalists. She supervised the publication of an official biography and donated a plantation to be used as a state park in his memory. Only in her final years did she shrug off the burden of her name and call herself "Imogene." Though Ura did not exist, Ima did have three brothers: Will, Mike, and Tom.

James Stephen Hogg was a model for the type of civic and state leader Ima was to become. Although his critics called him a demagogue, his friends knew him as a generous-hearted man whose genuine concerns extended to citizens of all classes. During his years as governor, he took Ima and her brothers on visits to numerous state hospitals and prisons; the images they saw instilled in them a compassion for the less fortunate. In Ima was born a special concern for those with mental illness who were lost inside those institutions. The governor also spoke up in support of the state university, the first Texas governor to do so. Perhaps because of the sincerity of his concerns, the Hogg children saw themselves almost as trustees of the wealth that his investments eventually produced, rather than simply the inheritors of a large fortune. They donated much of their money to causes that had been important to their father.

Ima's mother, Sarah Stinson Hogg, was the "civilizing force" in the Hogg household: a fastidious decorator and sensitive woman of culture, Ima's first piano teacher, and her ultimate role model. Ima was only thirteen when Sarah Hogg fell ill, and she was her mother's sole companion on her recuperative trips to Arkansas and Colorado. She even shared her mother's bed at night. Eventually it was discovered that her mother had tuberculosis, a much-feared, often fatal disease about which little was known at the time. After nearly a year of struggle, Sarah Hogg passed away in Colorado in 1895.

In the weeks after her mother's death, Ima had a fateful conversation with the aunt who had come to stay with the family. Aunt Fannie's husband had died from tuberculosis while she was pregnant with a son who later suffered the same fate. Inferring from

Ima Hogg, age seventy-two

this dual tragedy that a susceptibility to the disease could be inherited, Fannie implored Ima never to marry, never to put any children she might have at risk. Although Aunt Fannie's prim style of household management was an easy target for the Hogg children's mockery, this misinformation may have caused Ima to make a silent resolution. She once boasted to a friend that she had rejected marriage proposals from more than thirty different men.

Fortunately, throughout her youth and much of her adult life, Ima had three robust and like-minded companions in her brothers. Will was considerably older; later, he looked after the family's financial affairs and helped to facilitate Ima's desire to contribute to the public good. Mike and Tom were Ima's rough-and-tumble chums. Together they slid down the banister of the governor's mansion, romped through the rooms, and played with their menagerie of dogs, cats, horses, parrots, and ostriches. Later, when she was a glamorous coed at the University of Texas (UT), they would shoo away the numerous suitors attracted by her poise and charm.

After two years at UT, Ima left college to study piano at New York's National Conservatory of Music; afterward she returned to Texas to play music, ride horses, and indulge in just enough dancing and socializing to upset her father. Her life was rich and full. Then, early in 1905, James Stephen Hogg was seriously injured in a train collision. Through several operations and a humid summer of partial recoveries, Ima stayed by his side, traveling with him to Colorado, as she had with her mother. Her care enabled him to conduct his business affairs, but ultimately nothing availed, and he died in March of the following year.

Then Ima's family burdens perhaps caught up with her. Little is known of her life during the years 1907–1909, when she studied piano in Europe with an Austrian master. A photograph of a handsome German man found posthumously among her belongings may provide a silent clue to her frequent trips to Germany. It may also uncover the source of a three-year period of severe depression Ima suffered following World War I. When she emerged from this illness, the family fortune was secure, thanks to the oil found on their property, and Ima soon would discover her role as Texas's cultural patron.

Miss Ima, as she was known to almost everyone, was a talented piano player and could have become a concert pianist, but this was never her goal. She played and practiced, she said, for her own pleasure. She taught piano and involved herself in the cultural life of Houston. She joined a Belgian musician friend in planning a professional symphony for Houston, such as those in New York and Philadelphia. Friends described her as a tireless "pavement pounder" as she trudged through the city collecting $25 sponsorships for the symphony's first season.

The first concert of the new orchestra reveals something of Miss Ima's spirit. The program began with Mozart and ended with a rendition of "Dixie." Although Ima loved fine things, she could not tolerate snobbery. Decades later, she articulated her vision more specifically: If the symphony was "to qualify as an instrument of brotherhood," it must not be "aloof or exclusive . . . I must say it has ever been the aim of the symphony to serve as a unifying and democratic agency in our region and our city."

Indeed, Ima was attuned to popular trends in music and the arts. She composed dissonant music long before jazz artists made it avant-garde, and later in her life she embraced the Beatles. She snapped up Picassos and Chagalls, Matisses and Modiglianis before they became icons of modern art, and she built an impressive American Indian art collection. As one acquaintance described it, "She stays mentally young." Another put it, "She stays on the bus!"

Further evidence of her progressive, farsighted vision was her decision in the late 1930s to use her brother Will's estate and some of her own money to create the Hogg Foundation for Mental Health at the University of Texas. The foundation focuses on mental health—then, it was called mental "hygiene"—as opposed to mental illness and its grim institutions. Ima's unswerving pragmatism held sway over the foundation's work. For instance, she was reluctant to fund research that did not make immediate improvements in people's lives. She would rather fund ten community centers than build an administrative facility. The Hogg Foundation was designed to be flexible and to serve all Texans. It remains a major funder of culturally appropriate programs for Texas's minority and disadvantaged youth populations.

Ima clearly always saw minority and disadvantaged Texans as deserving the best the state had to offer. In her term on the Houston schoolboard in the mid-1940s, she worked to create a fine-arts program in the district's African American schools. She created the

Houston Child Guidance Center for disadvantaged youth. And she provided funds, as had her father and brothers, for impoverished students to develop their talents in college or music school.

Once Ima awoke to find an intruder rummaging through her bureau for jewels.

"Why are you taking my jewelry?" Miss Ima asked.

The bewildered intruder stammered that he was broke and out of work and had hoped to sell the jewelry to feed his family.

"Well, you're going about it the wrong way," said Ima. "Why didn't you just come and tell us?" Finding a pad and pencil, she wrote down an address and the name of a person who could give him a job that day.

Ima Hogg's signature contribution to Texas was her collection of fine antiques. During her recovery from depression, she purchased her first American piece. Her brother Will had arranged for her to sit for the portrait artist Wayman Adams in New York. While at the artist's apartment, she admired his Queen Anne chair, marveling that a work of such fine craftsmanship had been made during our country's pre-Revolutionary era. When Adams would not part with his chair, she and Will visited a shop where they found an identical chair in even better condition. It seemed prohibitively expensive, even for a family that had just struck oil, but Ima took the long view. She turned to her brother and said, "We have a rare opportunity—to collect American antiques for a museum in Texas. It's never been done before."

Thus, with the purchase of her first American antique, the vision of what would become "Bayou Bend" began to form. During the antiquing heydays of the 1920s, she made fast friendships with Henry DuPont and Katherine Murphy, two of the nation's greatest collectors, and earned the respect of New York dealers for her excellent taste and her fairness in distributing patronage among them.

Soon Ima and Will both had collected enough furniture to require a larger Houston residence. They commissioned a capacious house to be built on a fourteen-acre lot in an exclusive new Houston subdivision known as River Oaks. Will Hogg was the developer of the subdivision, but it was Ima who worked closely with the architect on their house. She chose a New Orleans-style pink stucco exterior, whereas the interior was designed to set off her New York and Philadelphia antiques. The green and blue paint hues chosen were vintage Colonial, and the hand-hewn floorboards were actually scavenged from Eastern Seaboard homes.

Ima lived in the manse from 1928 to 1965. The last of these years she spent meticulously preparing for the day when Bayou Bend would open its doors as an annex to Houston's Museum of Fine Arts. With a flair for decoration and an eye for detail, she loaded each of the rooms and suites with rare furnishings reflecting a particular historical style or theme. True to her vision, the internationally renowned collection presently exudes charm and accessibility as well as elegance, with nothing roped off or labeled DO NOT TOUCH.

Among many other awards in her life, Ima Hogg received the Rotary Club's Distinguished Citizen Award in 1969. The speaker described Ima's gifts as follows:

> History records many people who have earned distinction by their capacity to visualize and conceive constructive projects, others who have gained honor by their ability to carry out such projects, still others whose financial generosity in support of such projects has brought them widespread respect. Rare indeed, however, are those persons in whom all three of these essential proclivities are abundantly combined.

Ima went on to conceive of several other projects of permanent value for Texas residents and visitors, including the Varner Plantation House, which was filled with Texas memorabilia, and the Round Top Cultural Center, which serves at present as the site of festive, outdoor folk-music gatherings as well as a museum of German settler culture.

Ima Hogg only grew younger with age, it seemed. Besides enjoying the Beatles, she once complimented a young man on his long hair and got into an hour-long conversation with him about John Cage. At a farming symposium at Round Top, she showed up declaring, "I want to learn how to mow hay." This woman who had, as she said, "a burning desire to see something encouraging happen," was always one to make her own hay while the sun shone. And despite her periods of darkness, the sun shone on Ima for ninety-two years.

JESSIE DANIEL AMES

1883–1972

Antilynching Crusader

$\mathcal{I}$n April 1924 forty-one-year-old Jessie Daniel Ames faced the most challenging speaking engagement of her life. As a volunteer for the Commission on Interracial Cooperation (CIC), Jessie had talked to countless people—starting with her female friends from the suffrage movement—about the problem of racism in Texas. Her dedication and competence could not be ignored, and in January the CIC had rewarded her with a salaried job as regional women's organizer.

But a lot of people in the South weren't ready to hear Jessie's message. People in her hometown of Georgetown had called her names and sent her ugly hate mail. Her most virulent opponents were members of the Ku Klux Klan, a white supremacist organization that used violence to keep African Americans demoralized. After World War I this group had surged into power all across the South and had a lot of sway over the Democratic Party. Texas was no exception. Later in 1924, at the National Democratic Convention, the Texas delegation supported the Klan's candidate for president.

Jessie Daniel Ames

Jessie was going to speak in Mississippi, one of the most Klan-dominated states of them all. She knew her audience of Mississippi Women's Club members included more than a couple Klan supporters. To add to the pressure, the woman who had invited Jessie to speak was her older sister, Lulu Daniel Hardy. During their youth Lulu had been their father's obvious favorite. She was now the happy and influential wife of the president of a Mississippi military academy and mistress to a large staff of servants. In stark contrast Jessie's adult life had been filled with hardship; her husband's early death had left her strapped for cash and a single mother of three.

No record exists of the words Jessie spoke to the elite white women of Mississippi that day. By her own account worried sick, she had prepared extensively, but when the time came, "I discarded my three speeches, rose up when I was introduced and spoke for thirty-five minutes." Her talk probably stressed how the fates of blacks and whites were intertwined. Many of these women had domestic servants. As tactfully as possible, Jessie would have asserted that Negroes needed improved education and living conditions if they were to become effective members of society. She would have implied that these ladies could improve their households by improving the lot of their servants.

Later in Jessie's career she told her followers to "tie up" any speech they gave with the subject of lynching. In Mississippi alone hundreds of black men had been savagely killed by mobs claiming to defend white women's virtue and honor. Jessie looked coldly on the idea that women needed this protection, even as she recognized its sway among Southern women. Though Jessie might not have broached this topic in 1924, her message of interracial cooperation that day was persuasive. She received hearty applause, and after her visit, the women of Mississippi formed an interracial committee of their own.

The region in which Jessie Daniel grew up was no stranger to racial violence, either. She was born in rural East Texas in 1883 and later moved with her family to Overton, near Tyler. When Jessie was eleven, and again when she was thirteen, black men accused of crimes were executed by local mobs before the court could try their cases. Jessie later would recall listening in confused horror while the family's hired hands spoke of a victim blinded by a red-hot iron.

Jessie's childhood in Overton was stressful for other, more immediate reasons. Her parents had come to Texas without money or family ties. Both of them worked, her mother as a nurse for the town doctor, her father as a railroad dispatcher. Together they earned a modest income, but they never really joined the life of the small town. Her father, James Daniel, took a special pride in his "Yankee" outsider status, proclaiming atheism in a place where religious revivals were the summer's high point. Thus, Jessie's childhood friends were among the poorest of the poor. That itself would have been fine with her, she later said, except that they sometimes died from diphtheria, smallpox, or typhoid.

Worst of all for the introspective child was her role in the family drama. Both parents were high-strung and argued frequently. The third of four children, Jessie felt especially unloved by her domineering father. When Lulu, the eldest, enrolled at Southwestern College, her father insisted that the whole family move to Georgetown to be near her. Later, when Jessie entered the college, she was forced to wear Lulu's discarded clothes and was kept from attending parties. Still, Jessie admired her father and aimed to please him. Indeed, her lifelong distance from religion (both her mother and sister were unapologetically Methodist) was probably attributable to him. Jessie graduated from Southwestern College in 1902 with a Bachelor of Art's degree.

Jessie's marriage to Roger Ames, a respectable army surgeon, might have seemed to Jessie a way to escape from her family.

Unfortunately, Roger did little to persuade his family to accept his "socially inferior" bride. He may have had second thoughts himself. Jessie's visits to his overseas posts were brief; she often left with a feeling of rejection. She and her growing brood found refuge in Lulu's home during this time, but her sister's happiness probably added to her silent rancor.

By 1914, when Roger Ames passed away, Jessie's mother was also a widow. Jessie and her three children moved into the Georgetown household. Together she and her mother managed the telephone business James Daniel had left behind. Jessie found it more socially acceptable to be a widow than a rejected wife. Even more important, her role as office manager gave her a new self-assurance. A secretary described the time an irate customer came to the telephone company's office to complain. "If you were a man," he said to Jessie, "I would like to cuss you out." Jessie replied with cool condescension, "Now don't let that stop you. You just come in here and get it off your chest."

Jessie's interest in women's rights had taken root the first year of her marriage, when she found that she could not open a bank account without her husband's permission. Now, with her newfound financial independence, Jessie looked again at the status of women. Women who didn't have husbands were controlled by their bosses or by public opinion; women with husbands were controlled by them or by social custom.

Jessie herself didn't face either dilemma; she had no husband, she had no boss, and she didn't much care for public opinion. No one was better situated to speak up on the behalf of women than she. In 1916, when the Texas Equal Suffrage Association (ESA) called for local organizers, Jessie was the first in Georgetown to respond.

Jessie hosted the first Georgetown suffrage meeting in her house and was unanimously elected president of the local ESA organization. When the state ESA president, Minnie Fisher Cunningham, came to speak at a Georgetown meeting, Jessie immediately found a mentor. A political maven with her own place in Texas history, "Minnie Fish" encouraged Jessie to broaden her efforts. Jessie began a weekly newspaper column and agreed to speak at statewide gatherings. Within a short time she was the third most influential woman in the state movement, behind Cunningham and Jane Y. McCallum, a lifelong rival.

The story of Texas women's first vote is one Jessie Ames loved to tell. After the suffragettes had helped impeach the crooked Governor James Ferguson in 1916, the stage was set for a bill enabling women to vote in Texas primaries. At that time Texas was a one-party state; voting in the Democratic primary was more important than voting in the general election.

The bill passed in the state legislature and was signed into law by the new governor, William P. Hobby. The catch was that the law did not take effect for ninety days, leaving the women only two weeks to register to vote before the deadline. Complicating matters was the deceitful promise by county officials to send representatives to the precincts to register women. The law plainly stated that women must register "in their own hand" at the county courthouse.

Jessie and her fellow suffragettes knew the law word for word. They organized a "get-out-the-vote drive to end all drives." Nearly four-thousand women in Jessie's home county came "by wagon, by hack, by foot" to register. Jessie exulted at seeing women get together to "compare ideas on politics and candidates not clothes or recipes." She then helped to coordinate the intensive voter education that followed. With the women's vote firmly aligned on primary day, a slate of progressive Democrats swept out the reactionary candidates.

Then came the week in June 1919 when the Texas legislature was poised to ratify the Nineteenth Amendment. Because most members of the senate were in favor of women's suffrage, the opposing senators decided to leave town to deny a quorum—the number of legislators required for a binding vote. Catching wind of this plan, the suffragettes and their friends in the senate were waiting at the Austin train station to send the deserters back to work. The vote was cast, and Texas ratified the amendment—the first state in the South to do so.

Throughout the years the fundamental opposition to female suffrage had centered around "the cult of true womanhood," which said that women should not soil their hems in the cesspools of business and politics; their true force should be felt in the home. This Victorian ideal was eroding as more and more women entered the workforce, but another objection to suffrage had arisen in the South. If white women could vote, then why not black women? This was unthinkable to many of those whose daily needs and wants were carried out by low-paid black women servants.

In its final phase, when Jessie joined it, the suffrage movement understood the conservative nature of public opinion. It had long since ceased being the equal rights movement founded by Susan B. Anthony and Elizabeth Cady Stanton—a movement of high ideals and noble convictions. Now, more than seventy years later, it was focused on a single goal: women's suffrage. Jessie's ideals matched those of the movement's founders, but she was competitive and wanted to win, by whatever strategy worked, so she adopted the more conservative approach prevalent in the South. Jessie had truly found her niche in politics.

Thus, she was part of the latter-day suffrage campaign, led by Carrie Chapman Catt, which suggested that whites had nothing to fear from women's suffrage because there "were more of us than them." In Texas the ESA had also promoted a poll tax to keep "undesirables" from voting, and in 1918 the Texas legislature enacted such a tax "in the event of the ratification of the Nineteenth

Amendment." After ratification, Jessie helped organize a drive to help middle-class women to pay this poll tax so that they could vote. She kept to herself her dislike for its racist objectives; it was all part of her job as the president of the newly formed Texas League of Women Voters (TLWV).

Jessie was simply following the lead of the National League of Women Voters, organized by Catt to continue the cause of women's participation in the political system. The organization's stance was squarely middle-class, nonpartisan, and antiimmigration; it promoted such measures as English-only ballots and refrained from entering campaigns, even when one of the candidates represented the Klan. Serving as the president of the Texas branch gave Jessie a chance to lead a statewide organization, something she had desperately wanted to do, and it helped define her lifelong mission of educating white, middle-class women for full and responsible citizenship. Soon, however, she would find other educational issues that reached far beyond the League's middle-class concerns.

Jessie's work branched out when the TLWV joined other Texas women's organizations to form a joint legislative council focused on issues such as maternity health, prison reform, school improvement, and Prohibition. The group of women reformers became known in Austin as the "Petticoat Lobby"; despite this not-so-subtle mockery, many of their measures were adopted.

Jessie's reform efforts with this group exposed her to shocking racial inequity. When touring the state's prisons, she found the conditions of black women so deplorable that she lobbied effectively for a state-funded center to train delinquent black girls. When touring the black schools in her county, she found them to be little more than shacks, with an average class size of ninety students. Immediately she set to work raising private funds to improve the schools' finances.

These were problems Jessie could address, and did. But the real problem was in people's attitudes, the same racial attitudes that had stood in the way of women's suffrage in the South. Jessie saw with growing discomfort how the progressive agenda excluded blacks in order to gain the support of more conservative voters. She concluded that "someone with enough background to do it" was going to have to address these attitudes head-on.

The Commission on Interracial Cooperation was an organization created to bring blacks and whites together to address the "peculiar situation" of the South. It was based in Atlanta, also a major headquarters for the Ku Klux Klan. In 1922 Jessie became the chair of the women's committee for the CIC's newly formed Texas branch. Galvanized at a meeting where three prominent black women exposed the injustice they suffered, Jessie dove into her work, acquiring a library of books on race relations and enrolling in University of Chicago extension courses in order to develop her thinking.

Although Jessie founded the Association of Southern Women to Prevent Lynching and remained its sole paid officer from 1930 to 1942, she did not author the critical analysis that became its hallmark. Decades earlier, Ida B. Wells had collected the data on lynchings that proved only a fraction were motivated by rape accusations, despite all the rhetoric about upholding white women's honor. In more recent times the black leaders of the National Association for the Advancement of Colored People (NAACP) had called on white women to condemn this travesty. But the moment for this mass protest had not yet come.

What Jessie did was to lay the groundwork necessary to make the most of the moment when it did gain popularity. As a state and regional organizer, she contacted and met hundreds of local officers of the Young Women's Christian Association (YWCA) and the Methodist Women's Missionary Council, the two legs of the women's interracial movement. These contacts generated countless speaking invitations. All of her life's experiences contributed to her skills as a speaker. Even the fact that she had heard about—if not attended—religious revivals caused her to speak in rousing sentences. At the same time she was aware of each group's ideological limits. Jessie wrote that her new job called for "all the tact, the brains, the training and the mentality which I have been accumulating. . . . My years of working with wild-eyed women and suave politicians have stood me in good stead."

In 1929 Jessie and her family moved to Atlanta so that she could accept a national position with the Commission on Interracial Cooperation. In October of that year, the stock market crash ushered in a period of extreme racial tension, especially among the rural poor. The number of lynching incidents spiked. Jessie asked the CIC director if she could devote all of her time to forming a women's organization focused solely on lynching. He agreed, and the Association of Southern Women to Prevent Lynching (ASWPL) was born.

From her self-education Jessie knew that lynching was as much a means of intimidation as it was anything else. Disputes over wages or economic conditions were the hidden cause of many lynchings. For many sharecroppers summer was the season of fear, not just because passions ran hot, but also because the cotton crop was planted and the harvest yet to come. A murmur of an accusation was enough to drive hardworking families away, leaving the spoils to the landowners. The ASWPL's literature highlighted these aspects of the dreadful crime. These facts helped change the minds of whites who had always assumed that lynchings were the result of righteous anger at crimes committed by blacks.

Lynchings were most common in rural regions, where Jessie's grassroots organizing proved her greatest strength: She reached out to women on a county-by-county basis. The organization kept a tight watch on potential eruptions of violence and contacted nearby ASWPL women when action was needed. The women spoke out for law and order. They worked with local sheriffs, encouraging them to do their jobs. As elected officers, these men often felt pressured to comply with the will of the voters, including the men who wanted to take punishment into their own hands. The women made sure to remind them that they, too, were voters.

Jessie also trained women to use their pens against lynching. She empowered them to conduct on-the-scene investigations of vigilante acts. She encouraged them to correspond closely with newspaper editors. Jessie herself addressed a convention of the Southern newspaper publishers, asking them to tone down their sensationalist language in reporting race-related crimes. A single inflammatory word could undo all the editorials the paper ever printed advocating due process of law.

By the end of the 1930s, Jessie's all-volunteer group had won national recognition and acclaim. She had collected endorsements from every major religious and civic women's group in the South. Her petitions had garnered almost 45,000 signatures, including some 1,300 from peace officers. The rest were the signatures of white women. Though she corresponded with black leaders like Mary McLeod Bethune, Jessie insisted from the start that her organization be whites-only. Her political instincts told her to take on one fight at a time.

In the end Jessie's caution failed her. In 1938 Jessie made national news by opposing a proposed bill to make lynching a federal crime. She feared such a law would only increase racial hostility in the "states' rights" South. But times had changed; the New Deal had made openly liberal views more acceptable. Many of her members disagreed with her, and the organization quietly crumbled. Jessie retreated to the hills of North Carolina; she later returned to Texas to live with her daughter.

Jessie Daniel Ames successfully raised three children, one of whom had infantile paralysis. After her prominent career ended, she lived on to witness the struggles and successes of the civil rights movement. But according to her biographer, Jacqueline Dowd Hall, her just recognition did not come until the women's movement of the 1960s and 1970s. Jessie had led women in rejecting the "crown of chivalry that has pressed upon us like a crown of thorns" and in taking up more empowering battles in the real world. And she had taught them to look beyond their self-interest, as well, to fight the battles that most needed to be fought.

Jessie Daniel Ames died in Austin, Texas, in 1972.

MARY LOUISE CECILIA "TEXAS" GUINAN
1884–1933

The Notorious Hostess

"Hello, suckers!" The big, brassy, peroxide-blond woman, draped with gaudy jewelry and caked with makeup, huskily greeted the crowd through the smoky haze that had already wrapped the tables into an exotic intimacy. Prohibition was in effect in New York, but "Tex," innovator of the nightclub scene, was out to entertain her customers as they slid into inebriation. Entertainment was not her sole purpose; she was also out to rake in their cash, as her trademark greeting suggested. Her well-oiled racket raised about $4,000 a week from the city slickers who seemed eager to pay $1.50 for a glass of ginger ale—at the time, equivalent to a few hours' wages! So let 'em, thought Tex. Give 'em a good time, and nobody would ask questions—except, of course, possibly the police.

Tex had the Texan gift of thinking big: "Exaggerate the world," she would say. "Dress up your lives with imagination . . . don't lose that purple mantle of illusion. It's worth more than the price of admission. . . ."

So Tex would tell a few jokes and chat with the customers, rather like today's late-night talk-show hosts—and late night was

Texas Guinan as the Western Girl in The Spitfire

about the time that her evenings began. She'd introduce her bevy of dancing girls, "Now how about a big hand for the little ladies?" She'd bring the biggest spenders onstage and ask for applause. She'd get to know people and give them whatever they wanted. And, sometimes, she'd tell stories about herself.

Later, she wrote about herself in her syndicated newspaper column:

> Altogether I had the happiest gayest sort of child-hood—between spanks—any young American could have. Roping steers and helping the boys round up the horses were chores which I learned at an early age. I wore pants like my brothers all day long, and except when caught and sent to school I was tearing around the ranch on a horse.
>
> That active outdoor life is responsible for my unusual good health and endurance at present. A city bred girl would never survive the arduous life I have led, and still lead.
>
> It was a glorious feeling to lope or gallop my pinto across miles of plains with the hot wind blowing my long yellow curls out in a straight line behind me. And it never occurred to me to be proud of my freedom at such a tender age. It simply seemed natural to ride. It was the life of the Texas plain.

One day, she claimed, she heard that Hank Miller's Wild West circus was coming to town. She decided to go and show the boys some tricks, and by the time she had finished putting her bronco, Pedro, through his paces, she'd been hired as a traveling performer. Between her shows, she said, she'd wander the grounds and study human nature, absorbing Barnum's business adage that "there's a sucker born every minute." The truth of this circus story is questionable because more scrupulous biographers have noted that Miller's circus didn't even exist when Tex was a girl.

Mary Louise Cecilia Guinan was born and raised in the great cattle-and-cotton crossroads town of Waco. She was 100 percent Irish; both her parents were Canadian-born children of immigrants. They had met in Colorado; the same love of adventure that had taken them there inspired a move to Texas. Michael Guinan was a half-successful merchant—ambitious and perhaps a touch too romantic for the trade. When his daughter was six, he lost his grocery to speculation. Bessie Guinan was a devout Catholic and a dedicated wife and mother, teaching "Mayme," as Tex was called growing up, the social graces. Bessie dressed her daughter in the voluminous female garments of late-1880s fashion, and Mayme, despite the emergence of her tomboy character, loved the fuss and bustle. The two were so devoted that the family took to calling the mother "Big Mayme," a sure sign of whose was the dominant character.

Although surrounded by cattle culture and people of the frontier, Mayme grew up in a town of twelve-thousand, not on her fantasized ranch. Her early escapades involved climbing trees with her younger brothers, not riding bareback on the plains. When she reached school age, her parents enrolled her in the local convent school, where she proved to be quite a handful. Outside school some of her favorite pranks included ordering bakery goods for fictitious customers and trying on shoes she had no intention of buying. Inside, the nuns were shocked by her frank and earthy talk. So notorious was she that some of the upper-crust parents of her classmates forbade their daughters to associate with her. Mayme indulged her imagination with stories of heroic girls. Once, so she said, she kidnapped a neighbor's baby so that she could "save" it from harm the way one of her book heroines had saved an infant—by taking it across the river in a leaky boat. The wooden washtub she used did indeed leak, but the swollen Brazos River behind her house ran so fast that both "heroine" and baby had to be rescued themselves.

Even her most skeptical biographer has reason to believe that she may have been involved with a circus. There is no arguing that Mayme was a fine horsewoman, as her later performances in silent films showed her to be. Circus interlude or not, by the time Mayme reached fourteen, Big Mayme had planned another destiny for her daughter. Motherhood was every woman's calling, Big Mayme thought, and the first step to motherhood was finding a man. One summer, Bessie Guinan took her daughter west to Idaho Springs, Colorado, to stay several months at her sister's house; another summer, they went to Anaconda, Montana, to visit another set of relatives. Mayme enjoyed great success in these social training grounds. According to one Anaconda miner's tale, she "glorified in her swarm of beaux . . . [she] was always very much in demand and Mother was always there." In 1900, the year Mayme turned sixteen, the family moved permanently to Denver. There, according to the Denver Post, she "stormed the social fort and gained admission." She became known for wearing evening gowns to Sunday church services; at the same time she was gaining attention for her roles in local theater productions. But before Mayme's theatrical career could be properly launched, Big Mayme's influence won out: Her daughter married a Mr. John J. Moynahan and moved with him to Chicago.

Within two years the irrepressible Mayme had left "Moy" to pursue her dreams in New York City, counting on her talent and her big personality to forge an entertainment career. She didn't have much trouble finding success. One person whom she attracted was Hannah Boyer, an African American laundress who "borrowed" her wealthy customers' dresses to keep her friend looking snazzy.

Texas Guinan

Onstage, "Miss Guinan," as she was known to reviewers, capital-
ized on the reputation of her home state. One evening while she
was performing a vaudeville singing act as the "Lone Star Novelty,"
she noticed the prominent Broadway producer John Slocum in the
audience. As he rose to leave in the middle of a number, she
stopped and shone her flashlight on him. "If you're going out,
bring one back for me!" she declared. In fact, she never drank, but
the audience loved the gag. Slocum stayed; he too was hooked, and
he took over management of her career. It was he who shaped her
as "Texas Guinan" and pampered her and coached her to think like
a star.

A review from the *Los Angeles Times* of one of her Slocum show
tours provides a striking character sketch of a young woman over-
fond of attention:

> Miss Texas Guinan is in the budding prima donna stage.
> Her whimsical little egotisms are calling loudly for a
> strong stage manager to put an end to them. A pretty
> and vivacious girl, she loves the spotlight too much. She
> would make better use of her voice if she did not try for
> so many effects. And finally, she would appear to be
> more in the play if she would address herself more to
> the people of the stage and less to the front.

Tex, as she came to be known, was so insulted she insisted
that Slocum demand an apology. The critic, Julian Johnson, would
not hear of apologizing. Months later, when Tex was again in Los
Angeles, she recounted the story at a luncheon she was attending,
this time without Slocum. "If that Julian Johnson ever meets up
with me, he is in for some hard luck," she told her unknown lunch
partner. The man sitting across from her laughed and invited her
to dinner. After he had left, the host informed Tex that her partner

had been none other than Julian Johnson. Tex laughed heartily. It was the beginning of a long, loving relationship, but the two never married.

Tex was just beginning to enjoy the financial rewards of stardom when she made an unwise business deal. Known for her battles with weight gain, she formed a partnership with a businessman to sell diet pills bearing her name. The man proved to be a fraud, and Tex lost much of what she had earned up to that point.

Before World War I the silent film was just gaining a foothold in the United States, and nowhere more than in Los Angeles, where Tex had a home with Johnson. After the war the industry exploded as the new form of entertainment became very popular. Tex embraced it as a perfect vehicle for her public persona and eventually formed her own, short-lived production company. Her films were, of course, westerns, but Tex was a unique leading lady. Not for her were the traditional "damsel in distress" roles, but neither did she play wicked women or femmes fatales. Rather, she became the divided heroine—the woman who could ride, shoot, and rescue, but whose heart was as weak as any other woman's. This departure from convention became her special draw.

In the 1919 film *Girl of the Rancho,* one of the few Texas Guinan films now available on video, Tex plays an "orphaned" (fatherless) woman named Texas Carroll, whose cherished little sister is named Waco. When she rebuffs the romantic advances of a Mexican bandit, the Mexican and his friends kidnap Waco after tying up Tex and her mother. Having freed herself, she mounts her white horse and takes off after them. Meanwhile, a group of white cowboys has intercepted the bandits. Arriving at the scene of the showdown, Tex climbs a bluff with her pistol and lariat. The lead bandit threatens to kill Waco if the white cowboys shoot, but Tex is able to rope her sister and lift her from his clutches. The white men prevail, and in the final scene, their handsome leader gravitates toward the buxom, jowly heroine.

In a 1920 film, *The White Squaw,* a woman named Texas Caswell dreams of the West from the cabin she shares with her brother Tom. When the "revenooer," or lawman, shows up at their house accusing Tom of bootlegging, he takes offense and ties him to his horse backwards before sending him in the direction of the real bootleggers. But Tex worries for his safety and rides after him. She unties him and returns to the cabin, where the bootleggers have gathered in anger at Tom for his betrayal. Tex disguises herself in the clothing of a man she has shot and runs to join her brother in the cabin. Eventually, the lawman shows up with his men and sets things in order. At the end Tex only looks dreamily at him; then the film cuts to a family tableau of the lawman, Tex, and a young boy, their son.

After appearing in many movies, Tex eventually tired of "kissing horses in horse operas" and returned to New York in 1922. Prohibition had launched the era of the speakeasies—dark, basement-level clubs where liquor was available and patrons needed passwords to enter. At age thirty-eight Tex was about to create a new form of entertainment, the nightclub. Just for fun she began to bring her showbiz friends to Gypsyland, a Hungarian restaurant where her friend Joe Fejer had been hired to play violin. Word spread, and others flocked to enjoy the party. The owner of the Café des Beaux Arts saw how well Fejer and Tex worked together and hired them to host the evening entertainment at his restaurant.

Tex did exactly what her mother had taught her to do: Play the gracious hostess, make people feel relaxed. She greeted her guests by name, if she knew them, and learned their names if she didn't. Tex was the emcee, with help from Fejer and a few dancers, but the real entertainment was provided by whoever decided to show up. Soon, an ex-taxicab-driver-turned-rumrunner named Larry Fay approached Tex about forming a partnership and running their own club. The El Fay was born at the corner of Forty-fifth Street and Sixth Avenue.

Everyone came around, including news reporters looking for leads, looking for action. Literary types like Ring Lardner would show up. Claire Luce and others got their start there as dancers. And, of course, there were the suckers. Everyone there was a sucker; anyone who would pay the cover charge of $6.00 or more had to be. But nobody seemed to mind. "Hello, suckers," Tex would say, and they'd all warm up to her. Then there was the "big butter-and-egg man." Tex came up with this phrase to describe a big spender who distributed $50 bills to her girls. Every night he showed up, she would call him the "big butter-and-egg man." Soon others were vying for the honor.

Sometimes, of course, the cops came, sent folks home, and padlocked the doors. For several years it was a game of cat and mouse. One club would be shut down and another would open. Fay learned the loopholes of the law, keeping the liquor in a separate building and serving it only to regular customers. In response the New York Police Department gave its detectives enough cash to behave like big spenders, earn the club's trust, and then bust it. Then came the curfew laws: Places had to be closed at three o'clock, just when things were warming up at Tex's place. When the cops would show up, Tex would banter with them. The raids became just another part of the entertainment.

About this time Tex began writing an opinion column in the *New York Graphic,* a tabloid, and produced a Broadway show called *Padlocks of 1927.* In June of 1928 Tex's 300 Club was part of the biggest raid on nightclubs ever in New York. She was arrested and declared a public nuisance. During her trial she testified, probably truthfully, that she had never had a drop of alcohol and claimed she wouldn't know it if she saw it. Fay had indeed kept her out of the bootlegging side of the business. She described her job this way: "There was always something doing every minute. My duties were to see that everybody had a good time and that everything came off."

And in this case she got off. The jury was swayed by the fact that the accusing officers had attended the club for eight or twelve visits each, spending a total of $360 in taxpayer funds, though a couple of them professed not to like the scene. A huge celebration ensued the night Tex was acquitted. The celebration carried over to a film project, *Queen of the Night Clubs.* Her memoir, *My Life, and How!,* began syndication in the *New York Evening Standard.*

Texas's next adventure was a trip to Paris with her dancing girls. The other entertainers in Paris, probably worried about losing customers, agitated against her receiving a work permit. In effect her troupe was deported, but they returned home triumphant as the "Too Hot for Paris" Traveling Show and began to travel from club to club on a large bus. That tour was interrupted one evening when the legendary gangster Dutch Schultz showed up in Tex's dressing room and demanded she stop the performance. They'd had a run-in before her departure when she had fired a showgirl with whom Schultz was involved. The event was complicated by the fact that one of Schultz's men managed the club where they were supposed to perform. Tex quickly changed clubs, but this proved that it was getting to be a dangerous time for bootleggers and their associates. While Tex was abroad, Larry Fay, her former partner, had been murdered.

Toward the end Tex's life took an unexpected turn. She became obsessed with the noted evangelist Aimee Semple McPherson Hutton, and after a short debate with her on religion and women's role, Tex challenged her to another debate on a topic of Aimee's choice. The evangelist refused, but Tex persisted, offering to send the proceeds to a needy cause. The offer was typical of

Tex's spiritual work; while she brought a kind of joie de vivre to the rich, she frequently performed benefits for the poor. Meanwhile, Aimee's religious revivals were solidly aimed at the middle class. When Aimee's refusal proved firm, Tex went to her church, "got religion," and told the press of her sincere desire to preach. "I want to invest my time and efforts in spreading sunshine, happiness, and blessing to others. . . . Happiness is the goal of all human achievement and that is what I intend to tell the world."

On a rigorous West Coast vaudeville tour, intended to familiarize herself with the "sawdust trail" of evangelism and raise money for charity, Tex was afflicted with severe abdominal pain and consulted a doctor in Portland. Finally, in Tacoma, she found a pastor who would allow her to preach the following Sunday. She planned her sermon carefully, typing out notes. She knew from her years as an entertainer how little money and material success meant to people. What mattered, she knew, were the little, childish things and giving others the best one had. Sunday arrived and, as she climbed into the pulpit, she saw a note that said her mother and God were listening. She delivered her sermon and broke into tears. According to the pastor her performance left no doubts about the sincerity of her message.

A week later Texas Guinan died of ulcerative colitis in Vancouver, British Columbia. It was November 5, 1933, exactly one month before the repeal of the Eighteenth Amendment marked the end of Prohibition and the end of the era in which Tex had become a legend.

Tex Guinan's flamboyant character has been portrayed in any number of films. She was played by Betty Hutton in *The Incendiary Blonde* (1945), a film based loosely on her fictional autobiography. The popular 1961 film *Splendor in the Grass* features a short appearance by Tex, as impersonated by Phyllis Diller. Most recently, Tex was played by Courtney Love in the Martin Scorsese film *Hello Sucker.*

BESSIE COLEMAN

1893–1926

Flying for the Race

*T*hree girls sat at the feet of their older sister, who was reading a book under the light of an oil lamp. Ten-year-old Bessie Coleman read with the dramatic tones of the black Baptist preacher at the Waxahachie church the girls attended every Sunday. A natural performer, she often made her sisters laugh. But just as often—for instance, when she read about Harriet Tubman, who led so many slaves to freedom—Bessie's emotional voice made them tingle with awe.

Tonight Bessie was reading *Uncle Tom's Cabin.* Every day she looked forward to the story's continuation during the evening reading ritual. After all, she spent those days washing, cooking, gardening, and looking after Nilus and Georgia, her two youngest sisters. It had been only three years since her father, part Native American, had left for Oklahoma and the promise of full citizenship. Bessie's mother, Susan, an African American, had not wished to follow him into Indian country. Instead, she found a full-time housekeeping job to support her family, leaving the home chores to her eldest daughter.

Bessie Coleman

Bessie had received only scant instruction in the local one-room school. She had learned more from Susan, who never missed an opportunity to educate her children. Gradually, Bessie had taken over the night reading, and now was her moment of triumph. All eyes were turned toward her. She read the part where George Shelby tells his slaves how Uncle Tom has died, beaten to death by the cruel overseer. The book concludes with his announcement:

> It was on his grave, my friends, that I resolved, before God, that I would never own another slave, while it was possible to free him. . . . So, when you rejoice in your freedom, think that you owe it to that good old soul. . . . Think of your freedom, every time you see Uncle Tom's cabin; and let it be a memorial to put you all in mind to follow in his steps, and be honest and faithful and Christian as he was.

Bessie closed the book in a display of solemn piety. She scanned the faces of her captive audience. Then she broke the spell. "I'll never be a Topsy or an Uncle Tom!" she snorted.

It is part of slave folklore that Africans could fly—a glorious symbol for escaping life's harsh realities. In her role as the first black aviator, Bessie would come to symbolize just this kind of freedom for African Americans. Throughout her barnstorming career, Bessie constantly worked to "uplift the Negro race." Her ultimate goal was to open a flying school for people of color, who were categorically banned from U.S. aviation schools. As she once told a Houston newspaper, she wanted "to make Uncle Tom's cabin into a hangar."

Bessie was born in a dirt-floor cabin in Atlanta, Texas, on the Arkansas border, where her father, George Coleman, worked as a day laborer. She had five older siblings, but three had already moved away. When Bessie was two, her father brought the family to Waxahachie, the county seat of "the largest cotton-producing county in the U.S." They lived on a quarter acre of land on Mustang Creek, 4 miles from the town center, in a house George Coleman built himself.

For the poor folk of Waxahachie, Texas, harvest time meant long days in the hot sun with raw, bleeding fingers and a sack strapped to one's back. Young Bessie knew that she was destined for greater things than picking cotton. She lagged behind the rest of the family; once or twice she was even caught riding the sack of the picker in front of her. But she was spared discipline; as the one Coleman who could add, she had the important job of watching the foreman weigh their pick and calculate their pay. And, when she had the chance, she pressed her foot on the scale.

At seventeen Bessie left to attend college in Oklahoma. But after just one semester, the family's funds were depleted, and Bessie was forced to return home and work as a self-employed laundress. Every day for four years, the petite young woman would walk into town carrying a load of clean laundry and walk home with another load to wash. Along her endless rounds she was sometimes given a newspaper. Her favorite was the *Chicago Defender*, an African American newspaper brought to town by the porters on the trains.

Increasingly, the papers contained news of World War I. Another country had entered the war; another spy had been caught. Beside the headlines of U-boat attacks and the Battle of the Marne, there were reports of amazing new flying machines: the British and their Sopwith Camels, the "Red Baron" and his Fokker Triplane. In the *Defender* the opinion pages always attracted Bessie's attention. There, the editors boosted the South Side scene, boasting that in Chicago, one could find a decent-paying job among one's own people. Bessie's brothers had moved to Chicago years ago, and in 1915, she joined them. Within several years her mother and sisters followed.

After a brief course at a beauty school, Bessie was hired as a manicurist in the White Sox barbershop along State Street, the stretch where prominent African Americans went to see and be seen. With her copper-colored skin, high cheekbones, and vivacious laugh, Bessie herself was seen and noticed in the shop's front window, where she worked. Confident of her charms, Bessie was soon strolling State Street arm in arm with well-heeled gentlemen and dreaming of her prospects.

When the United States entered the war, Bessie's brothers Walter and John enlisted with the Eighth Army National Guard, an African American regiment. Two years later they returned from the front lines with a hoard of observations, one of their favorites being "the liberated French." The French, they said, didn't even know the meaning of racism. In France women had careers; French women even flew planes!

One fateful day John entered the barbershop intoxicated and proceeded to reminisce about his time in the service with anyone who cared to listen. As usual, the conversation turned to French women, with an invidious comparison to the women of the South Side. John turned to Bessie: "You nigger women ain't never goin' to fly. Not like those women I saw in France."

The barbershop customers might have guffawed, but Bessie was not to be put down. "That's it!" she said with rigid determination. "You just called it for me." She had decided to fly.

For advice about achieving this goal, Bessie contacted her friend Richard Abbott, the editor of the *Defender*. He was especially interested in how her story would boost race morale—and his newspaper's circulation. He recommended she go to France for instruction and promised to help any way he could. While Bessie took a hasty course in the French language, she buttonholed other well-off male friends, asking them to contribute to her cause. According to her family her suitors at this time included white and black, young and old, even a gentleman from Spain. Bessie must have been very persuasive, for in November 1920 she sailed for France.

Flying was then far more dangerous than it is at present. Bessie was turned away from a Paris aviation school because two women had recently fallen to their deaths. At the school where she finally enrolled, she witnessed an accident in which a male student pilot was killed. The open-cockpit Nieuport and Curtiss JN planes she flew were constructed of wood, canvas, wire, aluminum, steel, and glue. In her seven-month course, Bessie learned basic maneuvers and tricks such as "looping the loop." During this stunt the only thing keeping the flyer in the cockpit is a fastened seatbelt and centrifugal force.

In 1921 Bessie graduated from the school, the only woman in her class. She received an international flying license. This was two years before Amelia Earhart learned to fly. Only one African American, Eugene Bullard, already had a flying career; originally from Alabama, he had flown for France in the war.

Reporters from black newspapers greeted Bessie as a celebrity when she returned to the United States. She declared, "You have never lived until you have flown," and expressed her hope that young men of "the Race" would learn to fly. She exaggerated her own youth by five years or so and said she had ordered a plane from France, when in fact she could not afford one. The reporters were too taken with her dynamic beauty to doubt her veracity.

In the breathless months that followed, Bessie flew in a few air shows, gave any number of specious interviews, and continued to seek financial backers. Few were ready for her headstrong attitude, and she alienated many of those who could have created opportunities for her. In the most dramatic of these debacles, she walked out of a contract as lead actress in a film when she learned that her character started out as a ragged country girl arriving in the big city. Remembering with pain her cotton-picking past, she swore, "No Uncle Tom stuff for me!"

Bessie's aborted foray into film was a natural digression. In the 1920s pilots were part of a self-made entertainment industry. It would be a decade before passenger flights would become common; in the meantime, ex–World War I aviators who had found their life's passion in the sky found work in "flying circuses." Enterprising barnstormers arranged their own gigs by landing in pastures, negotiating with farmers, and pulling together audiences of a few dozen townspeople. Engine failure was not uncommon; many pilots crashed before their shocked spectators.

Bessie was at a disadvantage because she lacked the capital needed to purchase and maintain her own airplane. She also faced prejudice from the white press, which was reluctant to cover her despite the anomaly she posed as the world's only "Negro aviatrix." Hence, she lived on hope and half-truths, spreading sensational rumors about her accomplishments and future plans.

Her most celebrated triumph during this time came at a 1922 air show in Chicago's Checkerboard airdrome. Thousands turned out to see the local heroine so ballyhooed in Abbott's *Defender*. In a borrowed plane Bessie soared through a figure eight in honor of Chicago's Eighth Regiment. At the apex of the loop, she dove into a free fall, righting the plane at the last instant to circle the field for a final landing. While free falls were common barnstormer stunts, in this case the engine of her plane had actually stalled, and only luck had saved her. Wearing a dashing leather outfit, she walked off the field dazed and jubilant, into the arms of her family and friends from Chicago's South Side. Four months later, her second-hand jenny failed over Santa Monica as fans in Los Angeles awaited her arrival. Strangely, the disappointed crowd wasn't sympathetic; they were enraged! Bessie telegrammed from the hospital, "My faith in aviation and the [use] it will serve in fulfilling the destiny of my people isn't shaken at all."

Two years later, in May of 1925, Bessie commenced her most successful stretch of shows, a summer tour in her home state of Texas. Everything about this tour seemed providential, including the date of the opening show, June 19 or "Juneteenth," the day black Texans celebrate their freedom from slavery. Bessie inspired the Houston crowd with her free falls and barrel rolls. Afterward she took about seventy-five of Houston's bravest souls, mostly women, for bird's-eye views of their city. The same people who were not allowed to ride the morning train flew in an open cockpit plane! The local black newspaper, *Houston Informer,* proudly noted that this was "the first time the colored public of the South had been given the opportunity to fly." It was for moments like these that Bessie risked her life.

She was immediately booked to fly at Richmond for a Baptist Association meeting and back at Houston for a picnic of the railroad's African American employees. Then, on July 12, she flew again for the Houston public, this time charging for rides afterward. Between her show dates Bessie gave lectures encouraging black women in their struggles for equal rights and access to politics and education.

Bessie performed in San Antonio and Galveston and many towns too small to record the event. Everywhere she went, black families opened their houses to her. Back in Houston a woman scheduled to parachute from Bessie's plane lost her nerve; unwilling to disappoint the loyal Houston crowd, Bessie hired a friend to pilot the plane and jumped herself. In her hometown of Waxahachie, Bessie scored a victory against Jim Crow laws by refusing to perform unless blacks entered the same gate as whites. And the people of Wharton, Texas, loved her act so much that they raised money to help her buy her own plane.

Bessie went to Dallas's Love Field to shop for a used aircraft. There she found a jenny that suited her, but more important, she caught a brief glimpse of a world where race made no difference. Those who lived and worked at the airfield treated the black mechanic, Louis Manning, as one of the guys. They ate and socialized together, and whenever a stranger questioned the arrangement, they'd say, "We're all black people here!"

Bessie followed this Texas tour with a series of lectures in Georgia. She accompanied her lectures with film clips of her shows, always lamenting that African Americans were "so far behind the white Race" in aviation. She moved on to Florida, continuing to lecture at theaters. The Orlando Chamber of Commerce booked Bessie for a parachute jump, planning it as a show for whites. Here she scored yet another victory over Jim Crow. She not only demanded that blacks be allowed to attend as well, she insisted that planes fly over the city's African American neighborhoods to drop printed invitations.

In Orlando, too, Bessie glimpsed a peace she had rarely known. The Baptist Reverend and Mrs. Hezakiah Hill had met her at a lecture and invited her for a prolonged stay at their parsonage. The Hills kept an open dinner invitation for members of their congregation; at their table Bessie met dedicated church workers and schoolboard members of the community, people so very different from her friends in Chicago. During her days in Orlando, Bessie happily entertained the neighborhood children, hoping that they, too, would become "air-minded" or at least "uplift the Race." The faith of her childhood was renewed and, with it, her dream of an aviation school for blacks in the United States. She left for her last show in Jacksonville with the promise that she would return to Orlando to build on that dream.

Bessie's friendship with a white Orlando millionaire made it possible for her to pay the balance on the Love Field jenny she had selected. A Dallas man, William D. Wills, was to deliver the plane, which needed some mechanical work before it would be ready to fly. Wills arrived in Jacksonville with the plane three days before the show.

The next day, by a stunning coincidence, Bessie's entourage entered a Jacksonville restaurant where Robert Abbott, the *Chicago Defender* editor, was dining. With great fanfare she introduced him to her friends as "the man who gave me my chance." According to Bessie's sister Elois, Abbott expressed an instant distrust of Wills. If he did, Bessie shrugged it off.

On April 30, 1926, Wills took Bessie for a test ride in her plane above the field where she would perform. At 3,500 feet the plane suddenly accelerated, then took a nosedive. Witnesses said the plane began a tailspin at 1,000 feet. Bessie had left her seatbelt unfastened so that she could lean over and see the field. She had also neglected to wear a parachute, something she always did when she was at the helm of a plane. At 500 feet the plane flipped upside down, and Bessie's body hurtled to the ground. The plane landed on top of Wills and was ignited when Bessie's distraught manager lit a cigarette.

From the burned wreckage it was determined that whoever had serviced the plane had accidentally left a wrench in the engine. When the airplane climbed, the wrench had wedged against the controls. It was a typical accident for early-model planes. It was a tragic end for Bessie Coleman.

Bessie's life had been a chaotic drama of will and improvisation. She had seized on a purpose and pursued it in every way available to her. Eclipsing her unrealized dream of teaching African Americans to fly was her very capacity to dream so boldly. More than five-thousand people turned out for her funeral. She likely inspired thousands more to rise above the cotton fields and "fly" for the race.

BIBLIOGRAPHY

SARAH BOWMAN

Anderson, Greta. "The Great Western." *True West Magazine* (April 2001): 25–26.

Bee, Marge. "Sarah Bowman: The Bell of the U.S. Army." *American Western Magazine* (February 2001). Online: www.readthewest.com.

Christensen, Carol and Tom. *The U.S.–Mexican War.* Miami Lakes, Fla.: Bay Books, 1998.

Elliott, J. F. "The Great Western: Sarah Bowman, Mother and Mistress to the U.S. Army." *Journal of Arizona History* 30 (spring 1989): 1–26.

Miller, Ronald Dean. *Shady Ladies of the West.* Los Angeles: Westernlore, 1964.

Sandwich, Brian. *The Great Western: Legendary Lady of the Southwest.* El Paso: Texas Western Press, 1990.

MARTHA WHITE McWHIRTER

Garrison, George Pierce. "A Woman's Community in Texas." *Charities Review* (November 1983).

James, Eleanor. "Martha White McWhirter." *Women in Early Texas.* Edited by Evelyn M. Carrington. Austin: Jenkins Publishing Co., 1975.

———. "The Sanctificationists of Belton." *American West* (summer 1965): 65–73.

Johnson, Melissa. "Sanctified Sisters." *Texas Historian* (November 1974): 2–6.

Sokolow, Jayme, and Mary Ann Lamanna. "Women and Utopia: The Woman's Commonwealth of Belton, Texas." *Southwestern Historical Quarterly* 87 (April 1984): 371–92.

Werden, Frieda. "Martha White McWhirter and the Belton Sanctificationists." *Legendary Ladies of Texas.* Edited by Francis Edward Abernethy. Denton: University of North Texas Press, 1994.

CYNTHIA ANN PARKER

DeShields, James T. *Cynthia Ann Parker: The Story of Her Capture.* New York: Garland, 1976, reprint of 1886 edition.

Hacker, Margaret S. *Cynthia Ann Parker: The Life and the Legend.* El Paso: Texas Western Press, 1990.

Harston, J. Emmor. *Comanche Land.* San Antonio: Naylor Co., 1963.

Neeley, Bill. *The Last Comanche Chief: The Life and Times of Quanah Parker.* New York: John Wiley and Sons, 1995.

Plummer, Rachael. *Narrative of Twenty-One Months Servitude as a Prisoner among the Comanche Indians.* Austin: Jenkins Publishing Company, 1977.

Ramsay, Jack C., Jr. *Sunshine on the Prairie: The Story of Cynthia Ann Parker.* Austin: Eakin Press, 1990.

Wellman, Paul I. "Cynthia Ann Parker." *Chronicles of Oklahoma* 12, no. 2 (1934): 163–171.

MARY ANN "MOLLY" DYER GOODNIGHT

Crawford, Ann Fears, and Crystal Sasse Ragsdale. *Women in Texas.* Barnett, Tex.: Eakin Press, 1982.

Haley, J. Evetts. *Charles Goodnight: Cowman and Plainsman.* Norman: University of Oklahoma Press, 1949.

Hamner, Laura V. *Short Grass and Longhorns.* Norman: University of Oklahoma Press, 1943.

O'Rear, Sybil J. *Charles Goodnight: Pioneer Cowman.* Austin: Eakin Press, 1990.

Robertson, Pauline Durett and R. L. *Panhandle Pilgrimage.* Amarillo: Paramount Publishing Co., 1978.

Rogers, Mary Beth. *We Can Fly: Stories of Katherine Stinson and Other Gutsy Texas Women.* Austin: Ellen C. Temple, Publisher, 1983.

Warner, Phoebe Kerrick. "The Wife of a Pioneer Ranchman." *The Cattleman* 7 (March 1921): 65–71.

SOFIE HERZOG HUNTINGTON

Humphries, Flora. "Brazoria's Woman Doctor was One of South Texas' Most Noted Characters." *Houston Chronicle* (December 6, 1936).

Jones, Marie Beth. "The Doctor Was a Lady." Vertical file, Brazoria County Historical Museum, ca. 1960.

"Memorial to Brazoria Woman Doctor Would be Tribute to Picturesque, Self-sacrificing and Useful Career." 1925. Vertical file, Brazoria County Historical Museum.

Petrovich, Sandra M. "Dr. Sofie Herzog, Surgeon: A Woman Overcomes a Man's World." 1992. Vertical file, Brazoria County Historical Museum.

Rogers, Mary Beth. *We Can Fly: Stories of Katherine Stinson and Other Gutsy Texas Women.* Austin: Ellen C. Temple, Publisher, 1983.

Silverthorne, Elizabeth, and Geneva Fulgham. *Women Pioneers in Texas Medicine.* College Station: Texas A&M Press, 1997.

SARA ESTELA RAMIREZ

Cotera, Marta. *Diosa y Hembra: The History and Heritage of Chicanas in the U.S.* Austin: Information Systems Development, 1976.

Hernandez, Inés. "Sara Estela Ramirez." *Longman Anthology of Literature by Women: 1875–1975.* Edited by Marian Arkin and Barbara Shollar. New York: Longman, 1989.

———. "Sara Estela Ramirez: Sembradora." *Legacy* 6.1 (1989): 13–26.

———. Sara Estela Ramirez: *The Early Twentieth Century Texas–Mexican Poet.* Dissertation, University of Houston, 1984.

Tuck, Jim. "Josef Ortiz de Dominguez: A Politically Correct 'Corrector.' " *Mexico Connect.* Online: www.mexconnect.com/mex_/history/jtuck/jtjosefaortiz.html.

Zamora, Emilio Jr. "Sara Estela Ramirez: Una Rose Roja en el Movemiento." *Mexican Women in the United States: Struggles Past and Present.* Edited by Magdalena Mora and Adelaida R. del Castillo. Los Angeles: UCLA Chicano Studies Research Center Publications, 1980.

IMA HOGG

Bernhard, Virginia. *Ima Hogg: The Governor's Daughter.* Austin: Texas Monthly Press, 1984.

Fuermann, George. *Houston: Land of the Big Rich.* Garden City, N.Y.: Doubleday, 1951.

Iscoe, Louise K. *Ima Hogg, First Lady of Texas.* Austin: Hogg Foundation for Mental Health, 1976.

Rundell, Walter, Jr. *Early Texas Oil: A Photographic History, 1866–1936.* College Station: Texas A&M University Press, 1977.

Stillinger, Elizabeth. *The Antiquers.* New York: Alfred A. Knopf, 1980.

JESSIE DANIEL AMES

Ames, Jessie Daniel. *The Changing Character of Lynching.* Atlanta: Commission on Interracial Cooperation, 1942.

Brewer, Anita. "Suffragette Recalls her 1918 Vote Fight." *Austin American* (May 24, 1965): 24.

Crawford, Ann Fears, and Crystal Sasse Ragsdale. *Texas Women: Frontier to Future.* Austin: State House Press, 1998.

Green, Elna. " 'Ideals of Government, of Home, and of Women': The Ideology of Southern White Antisuffragism." In Virginia Bernhard et al. *Hidden Histories of Women in the New South.* Columbia: University of Missouri Press, 1994.

Hall, Jacqueline Dowd. *Revolt Against Chivalry: Jessie Daniel Ames and the Women's Campaign against Lynching.* Revised edition. New York: Columbia University Press, 1993.

Jessie Daniel Ames. File, Texas State Library, Austin, Texas.

NAACP. *Thirty Years of Lynching in the United States, 1889–1918.* New York: Arno Press, 1969.

Nieuwenhuizen, Patricia B. *Minnie Fisher Cunningham and Jane Y. McCallum: Leaders of Texas Women.* Senior thesis, University of Texas at Austin, 1982.

Winegarten, Ruthe, and Juding N. McArthur. *Citizens at Last: The Woman Suffrage Movement in Texas.* Austin: Ellen C. Temple, Publisher, 1987.

MARY LOUISE CECILIA "TEXAS" GUINAN

Berliner, Louise. *Texas Guinan.* Austin: University of Texas Press, 1993.

"Girl of the Rancho" (1919) and "White Squaw" (1920). *Western Heroines.* Phoenix, Ariz.: Grapevine Video, 1996.

Shirley, Glenn. *"Hello, Sucker!" The Story of Texas Guinan.* Austin: Eakin Press, 1989.

Trachtenberg, Leo. "Texas Guinan: Queen of the Night." *Urbanities* 8:2 (spring 1998). Online: www.city-journal.org.

Wallace, Patricia Ward. *A Spirit So Rare: A History of the Women of Waco.* Austin: Nortex, 1984.

BESSIE COLEMAN

Caidin, Martin. *Barnstorming.* New York: Duell, Sloan and Pearce, 1965.

Fisher, Lillian M. *Brave Bessie: Flying Free.* Dallas: Hendrick-Long Publishing Co., 1995.

Lomax, Judy. *Women of the Air.* London: John Murray, 1986.

Rich, Doris L. *Queen Bess: Daredevil Aviator.* Washington: Smithsonian Institution Press, 1993.

Robinson, P. J. "Queen Bess Flies Forever." *The Metro Herald* (Washington, D.C.) 6:16 (April 21, 1995): 1 ff.

INDEX

A

Abbott, Richard. *See* Coleman,
Bessie
Adair, John George, 36–37, 40
Adair, Cornelia, 36–37, 40
Ames, Jessie Daniel
Association of Southern Women
to Prevent Lynching, 81–84
birth of, 76
Commission on Interracial
Cooperation, 73, 81–82
death of, 84
marriage to Roger Ames, 76–77
and racial inequality, 73, 75–76,
79–81
Texas Equal Suffrage
Association, 77–79
Texas League of Women
Voters, 80
and women's suffrage, 73,
77–81, 84
Ames, Roger, 76–77
Anthony, Susan B., 79
Arriaga, Camilo, 58

B

Bethune, Mary McLeod, 83
Blackwell, Elizabeth, 46
Boujette, Sarah. *See* Bowman, Sarah
Bowman, Sarah
birth of, 2
bordello and restaurant
proprietress, 4, 6
career with army, 1–8

death of, 8
"The Great Western," 2, 4, 6
"Heroine of Fort Brown," 4
hotel proprietress, 8
marriages of, 6, 7
Bowman, Albert (husband), 7, 8
Boyer, Hannah, 89
Brown, Jacob, 4
Bullard, Eugene, 102

C

Camp Cooper, 28
Catt, Carrie Chapman, 79, 80
Central Hotel Company.
See McWhirter, Martha White
Chicago Defender, 100–101, 103, 106
Club Redención, 60
Coleman, Bessie
aviation, 99, 101–6
birth of, 99–100
as civil rights activist, 104, 105
death of, 106
and France, 101–2
in Orlando, 105–6
and racial prejudice, 103, 104,
105
and Richard Abbott, 101–2,
103, 106
Coleman, Elois (sister), 106
Coleman, George (father), 97,
99–100
Coleman, Georgia (sister), 97
Coleman, John (brother), 101
Coleman, Nilus (sister), 97

Coleman, Susan (mother), 97, 99
Coleman, Walter (brother), 101
Comanche Indians, 21, 23, 24,
    25–31, 34, 35, 36–37, 40
Cunningham, Minnie Fisher, 78

D

Daniel, James (father of Jessie
    Daniel Ames), 76, 77
Davis, Sarah. *See* Bowman, Sarah
de Dominguez, Doña Josefa
    Ortíz, 56
Diaz, Porfirio, 57, 58
Diller, Phyllis, 96
DuPont, Henry, 70
Duran, Juan, 7

E

Earhart, Amelia, 102
Eighteenth Amendment, 96
El Demócrata Fronterizo, 60
Enriquez, Andres Molina, 57

F

Fay, Larry. *See* Guinan, Mary Louise
    Cecilia "Texas"
Fejer, Joe, 93
Ferguson, James, 78
Ford, John S., 27
Fort Brown, 3
Fort Parker, 21, 23

G

Girl of the Rancho, 92–93
Goodnight, Charles, 30, 32, 34,
    35–36, 37, 38, 39–41
Goodnight, Mary Ann "Molly"
    Dyer
    as "Aunt Molly," 38, 41

birth of, 34
and buffalo, 32, 34, 37, 40, 41
conservation projects, 41
death of, 42
founding of Southern Methodist
    Church, 36
and Goodnight College, 41
and JA Ranch, 32, 36, 38,
    39–41
marriage to Charles Goodnight,
    35
"Mother of the Panhandle:
    Darling of the Plains," 38
as natural historian, 39
Guinan, Bessie (a.k.a. "Big Mayme,"
    mother), 88, 89
Guinan, Mary Louise Cecilia "Texas"
    arrest of, 94–95
    birth of, 88
    death of, 96
    early life, 88–89
    and evangelism, 95–96
    marriage to John J.
        Moynahan, 89
    and John Slocum, 91
    and Julian Johnson, 91–92
    and Larry Fay, 94–95
    and newspapers, 87, 94, 95
    in New York City, 85, 87, 89,
        91, 93–95
    and nightclub scene, 85, 87,
        93–95
    portrayal of, 96
    and Prohibition, 85, 93–95, 96
    theatrical and film career, 89,
        91–93, 94, 95
Guinan, Michael (father), 88
Guinan, Tex. *See* Guinan, Mary
    Louise Cecilia "Texas"

H

Hall, Jacqueline Dowd, 84

Hardy, Lulu Daniel (sister of Jessie Daniel Ames), 75, 76, 77

Hello Sucker, 96

Henry, John C., 16, 18

Herzog, August, 45–46

Herzog, Sofie. *See* Huntington, Sofie Herzog

Hobby, Wiliam P., 78

Hogg, Ima
age at death, 72
and antiques, 70–71
Bayou Bend, 70–71
birth of, 65
as civic leader, 66, 69–70, 71
and depression, 68
and marriage, 67
and mental health, 66, 69
and music, 68–69, 72
patron of culture, 65, 68, 69, 72

Hogg, James Stephen (father), 63, 65–66, 68

Hogg, Mike (brother), 67–68

Hogg, Sarah Stinson (mother), 66

Hogg, Tom (brother), 67–68

Hogg, Will (brother), 67, 69, 70–71

Houston Informer, 104

Huntington, Colonel Marion, 52

Huntington, Sofie Herzog
birth of, 45
chief surgeon of railway company, 45
and collections, 48–49
defiance of racial prejudice, 52
doctor, 43, 45–52
local legend, 48

marriage to Colonel Marion Huntington, 52
marriage to Dr. August Herzog, 45
medical training, 46
and museum, 52
as real estate mogul, 50–51

Hutton, Aimee Semple McPherson, 95–96

Hutton, Betty, 96

I

Idar, Jovita, 53–54, 55

Incendiary Blonde, The, 96

J

Jim Crow, 105

Johnson, Julian. *See* Guinan, Mary Louise Cecilia "Texas"

Juneteenth, 104

K

Kellogg, Elizabeth, 23, 25

Kiowa Indians, 21

Ku Klux Klan, 73, 75, 80, 81

L

La Crónica, 53, 55, 56, 60, 61

Lardner, Ring, 94

La Regeneración, 56, 58

Lincoln, George, 3, 5

Love, Courtney, 96

Luce, Claire, 94

M

Magón, Ricardo Flores. *See* Ramirez, Sara Estela

McCallum, Jane Y., 78

McWhirter, George, 12–13, 14,
    15, 17–18
McWhirter, Martha White
    arrest of, 16
    birth of, 12
    and celibacy, 13, 17, 20
    and Central Hotel Company, 18
    death of, 20
    and feminism, 12, 14
    and marriage, 14–15, 17
    marriage to George
        McWhirter, 12
    and religion, 9, 11–17, 20
    santification of, 11, 12
    and "Sanctified Sisters," 14–20
    violence toward, 16–17
    wealth of, 18–19
Methodist Women's Missionary
    Council, 81
Murphy, Katherine, 70
My Life, and How!, 95

N

National Association for the
    Advancement of Colored People
    (NAACP), 81
National League of Women
    Voters, 80
Naudah. *See* Parker, Cynthia Ann
New York Evening Standard, 95
New York Graphic, 94
Nineteenth Amendment, 78–80
Nocona, Peta, 27–28, 30

P

Padlocks of 1927, 94
Parker, Cynthia Ann (a.k.a.
    Naudah)
    birth of, 24

and children, 27, 28, 29, 30–31
Comanche duties, 25–26
and Comanche Indians, 23–30
and Comanche name, 25
death of, 30
and horses, 26
kidnapping of, 23–25
marriage to Peta Nocona, 27
and Pease River Massacre,
    28, 30
reunification with family, 28–30
and Texas Rangers, 27–28
Parker, Daniel (uncle), 24
Parker, Isaak (uncle), 28, 29
Parker, John (brother), 23
Parker, Lucy (mother), 21, 23
Parker, Quanah (son of Cynthia
    Ann Parker), 27, 31, 35, 39–40
Parker, Silas (brother), 29
Parker, Silas (father), 21, 23
Peenah (a.k.a. Pecos, son of
    Cynthia Ann Parker), 27, 30
"Petticoat Lobby," 80
Plain Account of Christian Perfection, 11
Plains Indians, 34
Plummer, Rachel (cousin of
    Cynthia Ann Parker), 23, 25
Prairie Flower. *See* Topsannah
Pratt, James, 23
Prell, Elfriede Marie (daughter of
    Sofie Herzog Huntington), 46,
    47, 50
Prell, Randolph, 46, 47–48, 49

Q

Queen of the Night Clubs, 95
Quohadi (band of Comanches),
    24, 25, 27, 31

R

Ramirez, Maria (sister), 54, 55,
Ramirez, Sara Estela
  and *Aurora,* 61
  birth of, 54–55
  death of, 53–54, 62
  and family, 54–55, 59
  and *La Corregidora,* 56, 60
  and Mexican revolutionary
    movement, 53, 55, 56–59, 60
  and *mutualismo,* 59
  as poet, 53, 54, 55–56, 57, 59,
    60–62
  and *Regeneración y Concordia,*
    57, 60
  and Ricardo Flores Magón,
    56–59
  as teacher, 53, 55, 57
Runnels, H. R., 27

S

Sanctificationists of Belton, 15
"Sanctified Sisters." *See* McWhirter,
  Martha White
Schultz, Dutch, 95
Scorsese, Martin, 96
Second Great Awakening, 11
Skinner, Nancy (adopted daughter
  of Sarah Bowman), 7, 8
Slocum, John. *See* Guinan, Mary
  Louise Cecilia "Texas"

Splendor in the Grass, 96
Stanton, Elizabeth Cady, 79

T

Taylor, Zachary, 1, 2, 3, 4, 5
Texas Company, The, 63
Texaco, 63
Texas Rangers, 21, 27–28, 35
Topsannah (daughter of Cynthia
  Ann Parker), 28, 29, 30
Treaty of Guadalupe Hidalgo, 5
Tubman, Harriet, 97

U

Uncle Tom's Cabin, 97, 99

W

Wells, Ida B., 81
Wesley, John, 11
White, Martha. *See* McWhirter,
  Martha White
White Squaw, The, 93
Wills, William D., 106
Women's College of Medicine, 46

Y

Young Women's Christian
  Association (YWCA), 81

ABOUT THE AUTHOR

Studying literature in college and then graduate school, Greta became aware of the power of stories—including true stories—to change people's lives. After a brief stint with poetry, she began writing articles for agricultural journals and educational publishers, as well as an occasional, heated letter to the editor. The More than Petticoats project gave her the chance to learn from ten remarkable mentors, to explore the vast and varied state of Texas—and to write, which has always been her first love. She teaches at Kirkwood Community College and lives with her partner, Paul, in Iowa City, where she enjoys gardening, splitting wood, and reading about a wide variety of topics.